The Age of Loneliness

Advance Praise for *The Age of Loneliness*

"In *The Age of Loneliness*, Laura Marris guides readers through specific ecological histories of absence-making: displacement, climate crisis, and the vanishing of species. 'The more a creature can tolerate, the more likely she is to end up alone in an increasingly hostile world,' she observes of herself and of the wildlife around her. Marris's critique succeeds through its specifically dystopian details: horseshoe crabs decimated for fertilizer, birds pulverized by airplanes, 'words from the living world' dropped from *The Oxford Junior Dictionary* in favor of 'database,' 'broadband,' 'committee.' This thoroughly researched, passionate, and courageous autobiographical nonfiction debut also reminds us that even in Western New York State's long history of toxicity, even in Buffalo-Niagara's now-desolate Love Canal, we remain connected by quiet ecosystems of companionship and love."

—**Susan Howe**

"*The Age of Loneliness* is a stunning book that will become a close friend, and like all good friends, it will change the shape of our world. Both personal and planetary, roving in its intelligence and deeply rooted in its lyrical observation, Laura Marris has managed that trickiest of feats: she brings the past into the present and reminds us that we're not yet alone. With prose that calls to mind the best in the tradition of nature writing, but with a voice which is also clearly, distinctly its own, Marris is the writer for our time."   —**Daegan Miller**

"Laura Marris blends memoir with reportage in essays of exquisite beauty, navigating personal and ecological loss. Are we living in the age of loneliness? the speaker asks, journeying between haunted landscapes—a lake named lost, an infamous New York Superfund, forests emptying of songbirds. 'I'm beginning to understand that absence itself could be a landmark. That sometimes, to know where you are, you have to navigate by what's not there.' *The Age of Loneliness* is an exploration of landscapes, interior and exterior, and the ways they become imprinted with both wounding and healing. As Marris reckons with the loneliness of late capitalism, what emerges is a work of love and connection."   —**Kathryn Savage**

The Age of Loneliness

ESSAYS

LAURA MARRIS

Graywolf Press

"Extremotolerance" first appeared in the *Believer*.

Excerpt from *A Handbook of Disappointed Fate* copyright © 2018 by Anne Boyer. Reprinted with permission from Ugly Duckling Press.

This publication is made possible, in part, by the voters of Minnesota through a Minnesota State Arts Board Operating Support grant, thanks to a legislative appropriation from the arts and cultural heritage fund. Significant support has also been provided by other generous contributions from foundations, corporations, and individuals. To these organizations and individuals we offer our heartfelt thanks.

Published by Graywolf Press
212 Third Avenue North, Suite 485
Minneapolis, Minnesota 55401

www.graywolfpress.org

Published in the United States of America
Printed in Canada

ISBN 978-1-64445-294-3 (paperback)
ISBN 978-1-64445-295-0 (ebook)

2 4 6 8 10 9 7 5 3

Library of Congress Control Number: 2023950734

Cover design: Adam Bohannon

Cover art: Prints and Photographs Division, Library of Congress, LC-USZC4-883

For the volunteers

It is a hallmark of our time in human history, that we think we are alone.

—Robin Wall Kimmerer

You hold a face in your eyes a lot and say "I am a citizen of longing for that one person," but what you really mean is that you are a citizen of longing for the world.

—Anne Boyer

Contents

The Age of Loneliness

1

Lost Lake

As we walk, I ask my father why the lake is called *lost*. To me, the place seems easy enough to spot—a shallow body of water curving behind the trees. We navigate a path along the rocky edge, a little disoriented until the woods fall away and we can see the blue of the sky returning in the brackish mirror. I've hiked this trail so many times I can't remember how old I am in this instance—seven, maybe eight—dawdling through Connecticut's Westwoods, close to where we live, an easy choice for a Saturday afternoon. The trees are bare, except for the scraps on last season's oak saplings, turned brittle and brown without falling. I put one foot in front of the other, watching out for heaves in the frost-thawed ground.

When my father starts to explain, his voice falls over my shoulders and I can almost see it like weather, shaping the atmosphere around me. As usual, he starts from the beginning. Or at least, he chooses a beginning, and I'm too young to question if that's where the story should start. This particular name came from settlers, surveyors, who stumbled on the lake, he says. When they began to map its edges, they didn't yet know about the small channel connecting it to the nearby marsh. This lake is saltwater, my father says. When tides ebb, it can disappear. He tells me that when the early surveyors tried to return to the lake, they thought they had lost it, because they came back at low tide. They wandered through the brambles and reeds, looking for the shoreline they had plotted, but it had become a meadow of salt grass—the edges were no longer the same. Impossible to get your bearings from a lake that doesn't stay put.

When we reach the overlook, the water is slack, shining in the sun. Clumps of reeds and islands, where rocks give way to lichen. My father hands me the sandwich he's carried, the bottle of cold tap water. I swing my legs over a ledge of granite, bounce the rubber heels of my sneakers off the stone. It's the season for cleaning up yards and burning leaves, and the breeze carries the smell of curled ash. There's a slight haze in the air, as there often is on warm February days, when nearby sea holds the heat of the land. But the soft edges in the distance also help with the sense of mystery. How does the lake fill through such a narrow gap? I ask. He says there are ways for water to move underground, too, that we see only some of its movements. But if you dig down you can find it, like with a deep enough hole at the beach.

Lost Lake is still drawn on the map, I say, even though it empties? And he nods. I'm beginning to understand that absence itself could be a landmark. That sometimes, to know where you are, you have to navigate by what's not there.

⌁

When I try to name my own relationship with somewhere like Lost Lake, the best word I have is landscape. Landscape, in this sense, is a word for the tension between human immersion and how that presence transfigures a place. It's not the picturesque or the wilderness or the "untouched." Even in the most casual sense, real-world landscapes are composed, characterized by humans, for aesthetic and political ends. And landscapes are also defined by what many people exclude from this careful framing—the shadow side of trash, toxins, histories of erasure, devastation, extractive practices that harm other beings. While environments and ecosystems are part of landscape, they also exist outside this framework, subverting human expectations through the sheer complexity of the living world. By contrast, a landscape is a human construction—a term for how each person's life has touched and entwined with the places they've known and how they carry traces of where they've been. As a result, landscapes are both collective context and deeply personal. It's possible, as historian Daegan Miller puts it, to "follow the landscape back into a person's mind and watch as she dreams it into being." At a moment when the living world is rapidly changing, I'm drawn to landscapes as flash points between what people perceive about a place and what gets edited out. They also beg the question: What am I not seeing?

A few years ago, I began to notice that I was editing out a specific category of experience. Though I was flying all the time for work, and spending part of each week away from the house I shared with my husband, Matt, I kept thinking I could pass through spaces of travel without being affected by them, without them leaving a mark on me. Whole days at the airport under the loudspeaker with earbuds jammed in my ears. Vistas of linoleum stretching for miles. Lyft rides in traffic on elevated highways—I'd never spent so much time in places people tried to get through on their way to somewhere else.

When I think of the airport, I think of the plateglass windows, how they bracket the sky you're about to enter. I've seen at least a hundred dusks turn blue in those windows. Until the darkness seeps across the horizon and the glass becomes a mirror, reflecting back the long passages of people, the crowds massing as they wait. At the airport you can feel the human and the neon jumbled together on the escalators, on the moving walkways, where you can watch yourself pass as though you were a package on a conveyor belt, funneled through space to reach the right barcode scanner, the one that opens the mouth of the gate.

One night, at the airport in a thunderstorm, I was waiting on a delayed flight. And I noticed that the water on the glass fell silently, unable to break through the noise of the terminal. I was longing to be somewhere else—to sleep in my own bed and wake up to the sound of rain on the roof. I wanted to walk away, into the drenched edges of the airfield, and think with my whole body and all its entanglements. To be somewhere (and someone) it was possible to touch.

This longing for the rain made me uncomfortable. It felt too much like loneliness, a feeling I reflexively repressed. In college, after my father died, I'd learned that it's dangerous to be lonely, to reveal, beneath the still surface, a deepening eddy of need. One reason I'd gone to school near him was so I could visit when he was sick, but I didn't expect him to be gone so quickly, to be wrapped so soon in the shadow-world of grief's associations, which were incomprehensible to most of the other nineteen-year-olds around me and which only exacerbated my sense that I was alone.

When he began to die, it was summer, and I was in France, trying to learn the language that would make me a translator. I got to the airport as quickly as I could. After the flight across the Atlantic, I rode to New Haven on the Amtrak train, whose tracks cross the narrow channel that feeds Lost Lake. For a few passing seconds I could see where we'd hiked as the inlet slipped through my pale reflection in the window. In the nights that followed, I stood by his bedside, thinking of the shallow water as the train crossed the trestle, rattling the conduits of salt. How I stood by the ebbing pool of his last conscious hours—when the tides changed and his hands rippled in the air as if to music—the firing of neurons at the edge of thought's dissolution.

Now when I ask the town historian about Lost Lake, he tells me that the railroad filled in some of the salt marsh when it built the tracks. The infrastructure for the bridge functioned like a dike, narrowing the channel and flooding the tidal meadow. So it was the train that created the lake. But no one I ask—not the head of the land trust, not the librarian in the town's archive, not the neighbors—can confirm the origin of the name.

When someone dies in a place and their relatives go on living there, that landscape is infused with their loss. I haven't set foot on the trail to Lost Lake since my father died—I no longer know what's going on in that particular corner of woods. Are the swamp maples still the first to turn in the fall? Does the winter wren still flex her sides to pour out her song, as if she could empty herself? During those long airport hours, I started to think about the loss of these other forms of kinship. If studies show that just being around other creatures and their habitats increases feelings of well-being in people, reduces stress, and relieves loneliness, what happens when the ease of that proximity is diminished, or altered, or made merely transactional?

Though most people think of the current era as the Anthropocene, the age of human impacts in the fossil record, there's another name circulating among artists and environmentalists like a warning, a name coined by the late biologist E. O. Wilson. In a time of great wildlife loss, when people and corporations have often pushed out other species to make space "by, for, and of ourselves," he prefers to call the coming age "the Eremocene, the Age of Loneliness."

In Greek, the word *eremos* can be applied to a lonely person, but it also means a desolated place. There's a doubleness to this lens, a reciprocity: when people monopolize a place, we often deprive ourselves of sharing it with the abundance of other living beings. "I have frequent conversations with students who have almost normalized this prospect," writes the author Robert Macfarlane; "they feel themselves involuntarily to be entering . . . 'The Age of Loneliness,' in which our depletion of more-than-human communities results in an emptied, echoing earth."

What I realized in the airport was that when I spent time in a lonely landscape, I instinctively felt it, and I just as instinctively pushed that feeling away. It alarmed me that I, too, had almost normalized the emptiness, for reasons that tangled with the personal, even as they went beyond it.

My long-distance habit predated Matt by four years and two different relationships. In grad school, through a Boston winter, I flew across the country alone because I wanted to keep dating someone who had moved away, someone I thought I loved. And how can you not fall in love, when your time together is a series of weekend vacations, escapes from the treeless streets of Allston and the long lights waiting to cross Commonwealth Ave? In between visits I would slip into a loneliness so quiet and cavernous that I hardly realized what was happening until its symptoms were clear. It became hard to eat when I was alone—all appetite gone, as if the hunger could only sustain itself by being answered and reflected in another person's company. Left to my own devices, I'd fall into a parallel world of dazed hours spent at the library, trying not to write about my father. I didn't want his absence to seep in and occupy this city, too. But it did, of course it did. I was his only child—wherever I lived, the shadow of his death caught up to me.

It's possible to forget an absence for a while if you cut yourself off from your places and how they remind you. Once, ice buried the

Northeast just before I was supposed to fly to San Francisco, where this then boyfriend lived, and I moved from window to window as I watched the plows, desperate for crews to clear the roads in time. Then, takeoff, the hours of suspension, the descent into a city where spring had already come in February and the branches were blooming with flowers whose names I didn't know. After four brief days of greenness, he tried to break up with me as we sat on the steps of his apartment drinking coffee, while the sun highlighted each barbed leaf of an aloe plant in its terra-cotta pot. I don't remember exactly what he said, only that the tones of his voice were measured, reasonable, gentle. Something like *Maybe our lives are going in different directions.* At first, his casualness stunned me. But as we waited for the BART train that would take me back to the airport, I realized that he had spent the whole weekend deliberating about it—while we basked in Dolores Park and ate takeout with our fingers, he'd been drafting this exit speech in his mind.

In the days that followed, I stopped contacting him, because I knew that space was the only thing we had that would fix us. I floated through days of dirty Boston snow until my friend Nell took me to the aquarium, where we stepped into a darkened room to watch moon jellies drift their iridescent cloverleafs through the tank. She took a picture of me standing in front of the glass, and in the photo you can see my shadow (my shade) behind me, looking like the more substantial half.

For me, living three thousand miles apart didn't mean we had to give up our love. A few nights a month in the same bed, the warmth of another coast—that was enough for me to keep going. The writer Hanif Abdurraqib says that to sleep next to someone is to "fall into the space that is mine and they fall into the space that is theirs and for a minute, there is a kingdom that we are keeping briefly warm and even if it is not love, it is love." I wanted a kingdom of warmth, even if it was a place I could only visit. I felt a loyalty to that kingdom, to that person, to our temporary country of non-loneliness. I even felt loyal to the way we missed each other when we were apart—missing as proof enough of affection. And for a little while, he relented and we stayed together, for almost the rest of that year. I paid my tithe in airport hours—and always showed up at the gate.

One of my professors in grad school put it well, probably after reading another bad poem I had written about getting on a plane. *Maybe you like long-distance relationships*, she said, *because you're accustomed to absence.*

"I am not sure what inner forces have made me, during the last years, ponder about and struggle with the psychiatric problems of loneliness," writes the psychoanalyst Frieda Fromm-Reichmann in an essay published in 1959. "I have found a strange fascination in thinking about it—and subsequently in attempting to break through the aloneness of thinking about loneliness by trying to communicate what I believe I have learned."

When Matt entered my life, my loneliness became less constant, less like a force that would swallow me, and more of a "strange fascination" that bloomed when we were apart. I could notice the curves and edges of the feeling, the slight pinch when it began, like the way Novocain aches as it gives way to numbness. If I play back Fromm-Reichmann's last sentence, "break through the aloneness of thinking about loneliness," I hear a familiar recursiveness, an uncomfortable wanting to share the sensations of this parallel world, even as it risks isolating you. When I said that it's dangerous to be lonely, this is what I meant—that trying to share loneliness, to talk about the vulnerability of that longing, always runs the risk of making people uncomfortable, as if it were a pathology, a contagion, and not a human response to living in a society that is often emotionally disconnected, ready to ignore a deep ache just because it might seem unfixable, or sad. When I feared my own loneliness, I suspect, it was partly because this hunger had spooked me when I'd encountered it in others. "Loneliness seems to be such a painful, frightening experience that people will do practically everything to avoid it," Fromm-Reichmann continues. But Matt didn't react like that. *I'm not afraid of your feelings*, he would say, and the openness of his face made my own fear recede.

When I confessed that I was having trouble falling asleep alone, he would tell me stories he'd made up over the course of the day, speaking into the phone until I finally surrendered my wakefulness, lulled by the sound of his voice. One story, early on, was about a boy who lives by himself in the woods next to a conveyor belt, like the people movers at the airport but longer, a moving walkway that stretches from horizon to horizon. Each day, the belt brings the boy new surprises—strangers, old car parts, raiders who want to take his farm. He builds walls, defenses, becomes expert at hiding when strangers arrive. Then, one morning, he decides to investigate and starts running on the moving walkway in the opposite direction, toward the source.

Fromm-Reichmann is right: most people would do practically anything to escape loneliness. At first, I thought the travel was just what Matt and I had to get through, to survive what academics call the two-body problem of being a couple without having jobs in the same place. I told myself I was flying so that someday, somewhere, we could live together in the space of fragile warmth we had created. I couldn't yet admit how much I needed the connections I hoped would share that space, the people and plants and animals, the world of associations, the projects completed and abandoned, the meshwork of collaborative metaphors. "I didn't want to grow older in a box, I wanted to grow older on a web," the writer Erica Berry puts it. The airports always hollowed me out but I kept moving through them, flinging small blue texts like balloons into his weather *hey, hi, how are you?* Little messages stitching the void.

In fields that depend on remote sensing, there is a concept called ground-truth. Meteorology and aviation rely on radar and mapping, but ground-truth is usually a human process—the need for people to find out, through firsthand observation, what's actually going on in a place. If a rainstorm was predicted, is it really pouring? There is a forecast or mapped reality, and then there is the ground-truth of Lost Lake's tidal shore.

Looking at it on the map, you would never know that Boston's airport is also a lost landscape. Before this place was runways, it was water: the sea between a brace of islands. The shoreline was an estuary, where tides reversed the flow of the creeks. In the spring the snowmelt would flood down into the marshes, and in winter, ice would pucker along the edges of the mudflats that are now disappeared. The wetlands under Logan were full of fish, herons, raccoons, deer. Three of the original islands—Bird, Governors, and Apple—are still buried beneath Logan's fill, as is a park called Wood Island, where families from the surrounding neighborhood dug clams, sunbathed, and dipped their feet in the harbor. Of course, as climate change causes sea levels to rise, the area around the airport has become wetter, marshier. The airport has developed a resiliency plan to safeguard its terminals, to avoid the creep of sea, to privilege the human ability to fly. But as Toni Morrison points out in her classic essay "The Site of Memory," filled land is prone to flooding, and water has a longer story than any human intervention. "'Floods' is the word they use," she writes, "but in fact it is not flooding; it is remembering. Remembering where it used to be. All water has a perfect memory and is forever trying to get back to where it was."

Once, I flew in a blizzard so bad that the air was as white as the runway. When the plane bounced on landing, I gripped the armrests because I thought it was turbulence, that we were still wrapped in cloud. And I knew Matt was on the other side of arrivals, one of the few people waiting for this handful of passengers who'd dared to board the only flight that got through. I walked outside, into the snow-filled wind that refracts its own brightness, even at night. And before I stepped into the car, I felt Matt's nearness in the wild air, how it filled me with such luck, such weightlessness to be buffeted down the sidewalk, to be both snowed in and in love. And also, as the car door closed and the air went still, how estranged, how divided to burn jet fuel through extreme weather—to accept that as people, the airport promised us connection, but as passengers we were isolated, cut off from every ecological reality of where we were and where we were going.

Biologist Robin Wall Kimmerer puts it like this: "As our human dominance of the world has grown, we have become more isolated, more lonely." I started to wonder if, in the Eremocene, loneliness could be a helpful feeling because it makes it harder to overlook what's missing. There's a strength—a stubbornness—to being lonely, to insisting on the importance of what's no longer there. To wonder why you never hear a certain bird anymore. To go on a summer road trip and hit only a couple of bugs. To realize, while passing a beach, that there used to be many more horseshoe crabs. To listen for spring peepers and hear just a few. Unlike grief, which is acute and often a response to finality, loneliness hums in the background, but if you tune in to its frequency, it can reveal something about the ways people have often become isolated from the living world. Loneliness is worth listening to because it longs for reconnection—a hurt that illuminates its antidote, a symptom that desires its cure.

To begin to notice ecological diminishment, even anecdotally, I had to pay attention to loneliness. I wanted to understand what it would be like to be a "citizen of longing," in the writer Anne Boyer's terms—to live alongside the losses in these landscapes in a way that might be helpful, real. And once I began to notice, I often found that I wasn't alone.

⌒

Each December, in places all across the US and around the world, small groups of people gather in parking lots and on lakeshores, armed with binoculars and spotting scopes. Many have been showing up for years on the same Sunday, in snow and rain, giving up their day off from other jobs to spend twenty-four hours counting birds. For a long time, these people have been known as citizen scientists, but now, for obvious reasons, people often call it community science instead. Each year, these cold, wet, wind-bedraggled volunteers gather population data for biologists and ecologists, comparing numbers of owls, or mockingbirds, or crossbills from one year to the next. People find both human and more-than-human community through these long days, searching with others for a particular species of concern, to tally the rise and fall of their numbers over time. In changing environments, community science projects helped me to be aware of shared loneliness as a feature of life that could be restorative, that could connect people who'd noticed the same something was missing and wanted to ground-truth their woods.

Many of my earliest experiences of the living world were shaped by my father, who participated in community science projects like these, especially when they involved looking for birds. When we walked in the woods, he would stop short, binoculars lifted, capturing me with his stillness. Then he would ask if I wanted to see. My small hands hinging the lenses closer, to fit the distance between a child's eyes. The black shadows at the edges of the circle, double vision until the adjustment was right. And then, a sharpness—distant wings brought close.

When he died, I found some of his bird lists from the eighties in the back of a folder, lists written out in longhand, with all the notes and cross-outs of a dedicated amateur. He didn't know that I'd keep them, that I'd try to retrace the paths that lead to their names. There are worse inheritances than a pile of bird lists and a map of Lost Lake I've drawn from memory, of a trail to a place whose shoreline doesn't hold.

2

Extremotolerance

True hunger for extremity is rare. Most animals that can survive in an extreme environment would prefer a less stressful one. Extremophiles—species that *thrive* in extremes—make up a much smaller percentage of life on earth, occupying places whose conditions would kill most other organisms. But beyond extremophilia, there is a second category: organisms who don't love extremes but manage to be exceptionally resilient. The tardigrade, for example, lives all across the world, from the tallest of the Himalayas to the abyssal deep. These micro-animals exist among us, functioning well in temperate environments, but several species can also withstand intense forms of harshness—freezing, aridity, toxic chemicals, radiation, lack of oxygen, salinity, pressure. Biologists refer to these tardigrades as extremotolerant.

When my long-distance commute was painful, when the traffic made me carsick enough to puke or left me stranded for a night on a bench at Logan Airport while rats cavorted through the garbage cans, I liked to think about tardigrades. Under the microscope, these animals look like eight-legged bears. Most are smaller than a millimeter. In their normal, active life cycle, they are vulnerable like other animals, but when they lie dormant, they can survive for years without food or water, suspending their metabolism so they require almost nothing. They can wait like this for the return of moisture, which allows them to once again forage and reproduce. Humans have irradiated them, tested them at subzero temperatures, and exposed them to the hard vacuum of outer space. Because of their barrel-chested shape, these creatures are also called water bears and moss piglets. They are often photographed under the microscope in poses that are vaguely cute, on slides of moisture scraped from leaf litter or damp gutters. But these "moss piglets" are far tougher than their nicknames—they have survived all five mass extinctions and will probably survive the sixth, the one we are experiencing now. These tiny organisms may well outlast us on this planet.

After emerging from the airport doors at some ungodly hour of the night, the first outdoor breath always felt like a drug, like a sheet of weather dissolving on my tongue. Even in the most human landscapes, we are always invisibly outnumbered, even among highways, taxis, great swaths of concrete elevated by the pillars of civil engineering, there is always the wind blowing off the water, the clouds teeming with microbial life, the hidden biodiversity of unfiltered air.

Though they are wingless, tardigrades can also fly. When they dry out, they can be blown for great distances, only to emerge from their latent state and thrive somewhere else. If they don't ride on the wind, they can travel as passengers, in films of water on the fur of animals, or on the feet of migratory birds.

In April 2019, tardigrades crashed on the moon when the privately funded Israeli lander *Beresheet* malfunctioned, exploding on impact. The payload, an object roughly the size of a DVD, included data about life on Earth, most of the contents of Wikipedia in English, human DNA samples, and dormant tardigrades encased in epoxy resin. According to the Arch Mission Foundation, which designed this "Lunar Library™," the resin might actually have helped the archive to survive the crash. These latent-state tardigrades in their protective coating were flung onto the surface of the moon near the impact site, causing some alarm for astrobiologists. Though it's unlikely that these dormant tardigrades survived there, planetary scientists still weren't thrilled that *Beresheet* and the Arch Mission Foundation inadvertently contaminated the moon with one of Earth's toughest species. Nova Spivack, Arch Mission's founder, told *Wired* that after the crash, "for the first 24 hours we were just in shock. We sort of expected that it would be successful. We knew there were risks but we didn't think the risks were that significant."

In a wild display of human hubris, "seeding" the moon with data and DNA was actually the idea. At the time, the slogan for the Arch Mission Foundation was "Humanity's Backup Plan." It was founded in 2015 as "a non-profit organization that maintains a backup of planet Earth, designed to continuously preserve and disseminate humanity's most important knowledge across time and space . . . preserving the knowledge and biology of our planet in a solar system–wide project called The Billion Year Archive."

The Arch Mission Foundation's trademarked (!) libraries are supposed to ensure that human civilization is never forgotten, that caches of data will be placed throughout the galaxy, wherever human technology has gone. Along the way, they made the generous idea of interplanetary communication sound more like a human-centric model focused on the preservation of our species— the planting of data flags on distant planets. Another one of their libraries was launched by Elon Musk in 2018 and is now orbiting the sun in the glove compartment of a cherry red Tesla Roadster, a hallowed piece of space trash Musk has threatened to suspend in orbit for the next several million years.

Is there anything some humans can't ruin? The question is tempting, but its nihilism is equally hubristic—there are many things humans don't have the power to ruin, including the geological processes of the Earth. At the time scale of an ice age, we wouldn't really know what ruin meant. As astrobiologist and planetary geologist Nathalie Cabrol told the writer Helen Macdonald, "It will survive whatever we throw at it. What is in danger is the environment that made us possible." On future Earth, be it a desert planet or a snowball, life will continue, just not necessarily for us, and not necessarily in a way most humans would recognize. As the climate changes and becomes more extreme, the species that do survive may become increasingly lonely. And the more a creature can tolerate, the more likely she is to end up alone in an increasingly hostile world.

When I met Matt, he was giving a talk about one of his artworks: an enclosure designed to feed and house a single tardigrade. The piece looked like an orb—one side held a glass bubble for the tardigrade, and the other held a digital avatar created in its image. You could interact with the avatar like a toy, a Tamagotchi, and the orb would simultaneously feed the tardigrade by squirting moss into the habitat with a long, thin needle. The avatar looked like a cartoon, with wiggling pixels for feet. Matt had named him Steven, giving him a Facebook profile and an email address. The project was designed to blur the boundary between conceptions of life and artificial life, to question the way humans anthropomorphize natural processes. But to me, the single micro-animal living in his orb looked like an image of ecological loneliness, a vision in miniature of the last animal alive in a small sphere, proliferating only through the simulacrum of a digital life.

Matt and I were both guests at an artist residency that winter, and each week brought a fresh blizzard. We walked down the paths between cabins as the snowdrifts grew taller, narrowing the gap between the pine trees and the ground. Matt lived in Michigan, near a series of trails that wound through the woods along a river. I lived in New York City. He was the youngest tenured professor in his department; I was a recent MFA graduate with three roommates and a psychopathic landlord. My relief at being in the woods, at escaping my apartment, was intense and more than a little tinged with grief. I was supposed to be writing, but most of my waking hours were spent missing people—my father, who had died seven years earlier; a close friend who had fallen into a deep depression; that boyfriend who had moved to San Francisco, and whose politics were sounding more and more entirely like the philosophy of Ayn Rand.

"I come as a guest / entering my own life," the poet Mary Oppen writes. In the atmosphere of the residency, I felt twenty-seven and threadbare, like at any moment the fabric of my life would rub away to reveal the skin. Or maybe there had never been any weave on the loom at all, and I had simply been shuttling back and forth across one set of threads until they broke.

Matt complicated all that. He made me pencil drawings of *Oculotrema hippopotami*, a tiny parasite that lives in hippopotamus eyes. Instead of screening art films, he invited all the residents to watch cartoons at the end of the day, making cones for popcorn from sheets of drawing paper. He brought me to his studio, where he was running a high-voltage current through a flame to turn it into a speaker. I watched the flame wobble as it talked, the tinny notes of voices expanding the flicker of the torch. Before we could think too much about it, we were spending whole days together in the library, a pile of books between us while the snow fell outside.

One afternoon, we sat there listening to clips from *The Golden Record* sent into space with NASA's *Voyager 1* and *2*. The record was launched in 1977, with an etched cover by Jon Lomberg, designed to give extraterrestrial life an idea of human anatomy and aesthetics. On his website, Lomberg refers to this kind of image-making as "'deep-time' communication." Along with these drawings, the record's tracks include music from around the world, greetings in different languages, and brain waves from the EEG of Ann Druyan, one of the researchers in charge of the project.

Before she recorded her brain waves, Druyan carefully planned a thought itinerary to include the ideas and mental images she wanted to send into space. But she had also just fallen in love. Two days before the recording, she and her colleague Carl Sagan had decided to get married over the course of a single phone call, without even going on a date. She called it their "*Eureka!* moment." For *Voyager*, Druyan's hour-long EEG was compressed into a minute and put on the record, a minute that, according to NASA's website, sounds like "a string of exploding firecrackers." "My feelings as a 27 year old woman, madly fallen in love, they're on that record," she later said. "It's forever. It'll be true 100 million years from now. For me Voyager is a kind of joy so powerful, it robs you of your fear of death."

I had the opposite reaction to falling in love at twenty-seven. Before I met Matt, I was more sanguine about dying, but our time together seemed, and still seems, so short. Fifty years? Sixty? It feels like Earth time—slow only on an individual scale, an illusion of suspension that belies our status as an eyeblink in the geological history of the planet. Our first year, we tried to spend as much time together as we could. When Matt was scheduled to give an artist talk in Reno, I decided to fly with him. After plummeting through gusts of desert wind, we sat outside in a pool of dry sunshine that made my skin prickle after the cold of the East Coast. We ordered beers to erase the turbulence of the flight and let the warmth of the day course through us, arguing about the benefits of enduring, the hunger for immortality.

I pointed out that despite our best efforts, permanence is always a gamble. The Svalbard Global Seed Vault, a repository for crop seeds from all over the world, describes itself as "the world's largest backup collection of seed samples." When smaller seed banks are destroyed through war, natural disasters, or mismanagement, this facility aims to preserve crop diversity through its collection, buried in a vault and kept at minus eighteen degrees Celsius. The Crop Trust organization calls this place "the ultimate insurance policy for the world's food supply. . . . offering options for future generations to overcome the challenges of climate change." Though this vault was opened by the Norwegian government in 2008 and designed to run without human intervention as a "doomsday" backup and a fail-safe, rising arctic temperatures have already revised that narrative. In 2017, permafrost thawed and caused a flood at the facility's entrance tunnel. Though the meltwater didn't reach the vault itself, the flood illustrates the vulnerability of fail-safes on a planet whose climate is rapidly changing. In less than ten years, this repository has already needed modifications like pumps and drainage conduits to make it more resilient to climate change— and it is supposed to last for centuries.

To me, even the space record's "'deep-time' communication" has its fallible side. Years after he made drawings for *Voyager*'s golden message, Jon Lomberg helped draft warning signs for the Department of Energy's Waste Isolation Pilot Plant in New Mexico, "the nation's only deep geologic long-lived radioactive waste repository." Located on a piece of desert called the Withdrawal, the WIPP's caverns store materials that have been contaminated by atomic bomb tests and the production of nuclear weapons. Once the repository is full, the plan is for markers to include warnings in seven languages. The design includes Navajo, Diné Bizaad, a Native language of the region, whose Indigenous inhabitants have borne the fallout from uranium mining and protested the exposure hazards of living near this site as it is filled.

Besides, reassurances about safety don't work so well when the facility itself plans to post the dangers for those who might come after.

As a pictographic message to beings of the future, atomic repository designers proposed a face like the one from Edvard Munch's *The Scream*. They also proposed cats that would change color when exposed to radiation, and the notorious "atomic priesthood"— a group of scientists and researchers who would pass down myths and superstitions about the area around the WIPP, so people would fear it for at least ten thousand years. These days, the plan calls for granite markers whose language will convey a message that "this place is not a place of honor . . . nothing valued is here." In short, the same man who immortalized visual communication for *Voyager* also helped to make an eternal biohazard sign. So often, what lasts is what can't be undone.

If these facilities are ever disturbed, some people reason that at least they won't be alive to see it. But as we finished our beers and walked through the empty storefronts and smoking sections of Reno, Matt told me he still wanted to escape death like a character in a movie, an ice zombie rescued from the deep freeze by intrepid scientists from the future. For him there was an optimism, a luck to persistence that he wasn't about to refuse. If permanence is a gamble, he asked, aren't you curious to see what adapts and heals and stays? I had always laughed at the deep-freeze idea. But for the first time, love set the fear of death loose on me. I wanted to linger, too.

When tardigrades enter their dormant state, it's called cryptobiosis. Their metabolism shuts down, their cells dry out, and they don't experience their normal processes of aging. In a favorable environment, some species of tardigrade can live anywhere from three months to two years, but they can survive in cryptobiosis for three decades. If tardigrades are exposed to harsh conditions like radiation, a protein called a damage suppressor may help to shield their DNA, preventing it from fracturing at high levels of radiation.

These creatures might seem passive in their toughness, but at the cellular level, they are fighting to survive.

One of the lessons of Matt's artwork *Tardigotchi* is that data alone isn't proof of life, or rather, it can only be proof that life once existed. The avatar of a tardigrade doesn't replace the unique future of the living creature's proteins. The world around the data ages into the oblivion of relentless change. Or, as the poet Susan Howe puts it, "Facts are perceptions of surfaces." And also, "Words are widows of thought." We catch just a partial story of the living world. But that doesn't make it any less profound to imagine the fossilized brain waves of a person deeply in love, banking slowly around the shadow side of a distant planet.

When the residency ended, I waited to see if Matt would go back to his old life. He waited to see if I would go back to mine. But it never really felt like a choice. A few weeks later, he came to see me in New York, booking flights on Spirit Airlines. We walked in Prospect Park as the paths of packed snow slowly turned into floods of meltwater that reflected the sky. Everything that had been buried in the winter drifts was emerging, coating the walkways with sand, gum wrappers, ChapSticks, pacifiers—all the small archaeologies of human passage. The day he left, he drew a flock of finches and stuck it in the frame of the window. Was loneliness our word for the shadow of resilience? It was easy to fall for a personifier of tardigrades, a man born under the sign of optimism, the same week as the launch of *Voyager 2*. We had no idea what our life together would look like if it wasn't at a distance, but when we were apart, the waiting was like a hollow under my collarbone, a holding pattern, a constant hunger for the smallest details of another human's life.

What doesn't kill you makes you stronger is one of the stupidest American expressions. Even at the level of the tardigrade, withstanding damage has its consequences. In one experiment, most of the tardigrades

exposed to the hard vacuum of space survived and even reproduced, but their mortality rate afterward was no better than the
control. Which means having a damage-suppressing protein that
protects your DNA isn't a ticket to immortality, but rather a way to
enter an altered state so that living doesn't kill you.

For humans, this kind of tolerance is dangerous because you can
passively persist in it while you wait for the world to change. In
summers that get progressively hotter, if you're lucky you can go
indoors and distance yourself from the physical effects of the heat,
turning up the AC and waiting for things to improve. And all the
while, the ecosystem around you (your ecosystem) is facing the full
force of these changes, year after year. While you enact your form of
resilience and wait, other living things are becoming more stressed,
and scarcer. As the sixth extinction progresses, biodiversity as we
know it is diminishing, and taking the stability of many ecosystems
with it. It would be better to say, *What doesn't kill us makes us lonelier.*

Neither Ann Druyan nor Carl Sagan believed in an afterlife. In
2003, Druyan wrote that people sometimes ask her if her husband changed his mind when he was dying, if he ever abandoned
his atheism to entertain the idea that they might see each other
again. She said the answer was no. All told, they had about twenty
years. Twenty years of collaboration, activism, parenthood. And
she is a widow now, engaged in the most intimate of long-distance
relationships—the interaction between a living mind and the memory of the dead.

3

Flat-Earthers

Circular thinking can be mistaken for instinct if you let it fester too much. Or commuting to see someone becomes the circle, and the thinking just follows suit: *We fly to see each other, because to see each other we have to fly.* In long-distance relationships, there can come a point when booking the travel is inescapable, when filling out the flight options and credit card information is like crossing a ruinous no-man's-land between the intense desire to see someone and the airline confirmation code. The mechanism for spanning the distance takes over, pushing away all other forms of reasoning. I know I wasn't alone in these obsessional patterns of thought. Once, a man I was dating long-distance asked me to clarify the future of our relationship, then hesitated: *Don't get me wrong*, he said. *I still love the loop.*

When we lived apart, Matt and I tried not to let air travel be the only conveyance that connected us. When our work allowed it, we shared our spaces for long, irregular stretches, bringing our problems, our projects, his elderly beagle (who soon became simply, our dog). Even so, I took every chance to escape what I saw as a deadening and circular pattern: *I'll visit your life, then you visit mine.* Once, when we were invited to a costume party, we decided to dress as the thing most unlike ourselves. For a night, we would be a pair of flat-earthers, people who believe the world is just a pancake ringed by ice, a disk whose edge gives way to the void. In our flat-earther outfits, the fronts of our T-shirts were screen-printed with foreshortened globes, narrowing our North American continent. The best part of the costume was that the Earth's flatness abbreviated the distance between our cities. We walked around all night as evangelists of the shortest line between two points, the embodiment of "as the crow flies."

When I was visiting him, Matt and I would take lunch breaks on the hill next to his art studio in Ann Arbor, Michigan. The hill was man-made and overlooked a thirty-two-acre expanse called Mcity, a name that was grander than its suburban reality. In truth, Mcity was a field with segments of road stretched across it and a few building facades, like the set of a Midwestern B movie. What did the *M* stand for? Michigan city? Model city? Motor? *Yes*, the big yellow *M* seemed to say, *anywhere and all of the above*. Like a facade without a building, the initial had no word. But they called it a city because it was an investment—a simulated road system for testing self-driving cars. The field beneath the hill was covered with tidy, well-behaved grass and sections of pavement painted with yellow lines. The landscape was mowed to keep the meadow from returning, so the cars could learn to recognize the boundaries of the road in a controlled environment. Its sidewalks included fake parking meters, mailboxes that went nowhere, ghost bikes owned by no one. There were also flat people at Mcity, painted cutouts that could be mistaken for shadows until you noticed that they, too, cast elongated shapes on the ground.

Self-driving cars were being trained to avoid hitting pedestrians here, so the person-shaped cutouts could be positioned at the edges of the roads, as if they were poised to step off a curb. These fake people could be thrust in front of cars, too, to test if they would stop. The roads in the field came from nowhere and went nowhere, turning in on themselves abruptly, as if they had reached the edge of a child's drawing. Asphalt is, of all things, recyclable, and Matt and I speculated about making an artwork that was just an endless piece of road being created before us and torn up behind us. As a performance, we would walk between the roller and the jackhammer through a deserted landscape. We dreamed of writing in chalk on that road before it was unmade, like the way you write a secret on a piece of paper and throw it into a fire.

We always wondered, during our picnics overlooking the field, if we would see the cars crash, if they would exceed the edges of their asphalt nursery. But the landscape was usually empty, with fewer birds than you might expect, and no bees to interrupt our lunches. The autonomous vehicles parked or rolled slowly, lingering behind a stop sign while a man with a laptop observed. The machines looked like they were learning to read—to distinguish a curve from a straightaway, to notice the reflective text on the highway sign, to stop when presented with a red hexagon. As these cars stored images of landmarks for future use, they were really being taught the elements of wayfinding, one of the most basic reasons humans commit the particulars of a landscape to memory. Watching these vehicles absorb their environment made me uneasy, though I didn't exactly know why.

At the time, Matt hated cars and didn't have one, even though it wasn't easy to live in Ann Arbor without driving. Leaving his studio, we would walk through the parks of the actual town, down the edges of bike trails, across athletic fields dotted with flat cutouts of coyotes to keep away the geese. The birds didn't stay away long, returning as soon as they realized they weren't being chased. And the flat coyotes were often in the position of running or howling, which made them look especially stupid—what coyote runs without moving? What animal would mistake a flat, black rictus for the living howl? It felt like all of Ann Arbor was full of cutouts silhouetted against a turbulent sky.

One morning before dawn, Matt finished a long stint of work at his studio. He'd been up all night and was too tired to walk home, so he called a Lyft. It was the least human hour in a college town, when raccoons lick foam out of discarded Solo cups, and panicked students abandon their keyboards to sleep for a few hours before their exams. Matt dozed in the back seat, through the center of campus, passing the mellow backlighting of the closed bars, the quad where flyers papered the ground. He was almost home when his Lyft was T-boned at a light by another car—the driver, apologetic, frantic, said he ran the red light because he was late for work at the Henry Ford Museum. The impact made a crater in the passenger side. The Lyft driver, who was uninjured, asked Matt if he should call him another Lyft. When Matt took a shocked breath, the pain doubled him over. *Just help me find my glasses.*

He arrived home on foot, limping as he fell into bed. In the light of day, Matt was mostly just sore and whiplashed, but his ribs on one side were pretty swollen. When I touched them, he flinched away from my hand, and I thought he should get them looked at. At the hospital, checking him in for X-rays, the staff refused to believe that he didn't have car insurance. When he told them he didn't have a car, they were perplexed—how was it possible that he taught at the university and didn't drive there? Did anyone in his household carry car insurance? Wasn't anyone in his family a driver? By Michigan law, they told him, all injuries from vehicles must be processed through car insurance. Nodding helpfully, as if to a child, an administrator spoke in the cajoling tone reserved for this kind of discussion. Matt told them he had health insurance, but they persisted for half an hour. The doctors went on with their work, and seemed to have no problem billing it all to his deluxe university health plan. On his way out the door, Matt realized the hospital insurance administrator had stapled his business card to the visit summary, just in case Matt had been mistaken. *If you were a pedestrian walking,* the man said, *we would still try to bill your car insurance. That's just how it is in Michigan.*

At the time, the state was dealing with the aftermath of Detroit's bankruptcy and the polarized forces of car culture and ruins photography, also known as ruin porn. "Urban explorers" were coming in to train their thousand-dollar lenses on Detroit parking garages and vacant lots, publishing images of "dystopian-chic" and peeling paint. The airport had a banner that read *Welcome to Detroit: The Comeback City.* Local activists protested, focusing on gentrification and outside investment as forces that destroyed neighborhoods and made them unlivable. Fledgling artists were often caught in the middle. Later, when I was teaching a graduate thesis workshop, an art student asked me how to write a ruin. It was an honest question. He wanted to know how to translate the disintegration he'd captured in his drawings into the medium of words on a page. The snow was coming down outside the window in April, and a pair of cardinals were perching in the leafless ivy that wrapped across the glass. *But wait,* I answered. *How do you know it's a ruin?*

Before the field by Matt's studio became Mcity, it was part of the Pfizer complex for research and development that helped to create Lipitor, one of the best-selling cholesterol drugs in US history. I remember the Lipitor commercials from my childhood—TV spots full of silver foxes, with the tag line *No body is perfect.* Doctors prescribed it as a wonder drug, a fountain of youth that could finally reverse the effects of the American diet. Lipitor came to make up a quarter of Pfizer's sales, and the Ann Arbor campus worked on a study called ILLUMINATE to create the follow-up drug, Torcetrapib. But the second drug failed to perform in clinical trials, and in the mid-2000s Pfizer cut its losses, closing down its entire Ann Arbor research facility. Residents of the town told stories of giant halls filled with empty monkey cages and desks stacked to the ceiling. One of Matt's colleagues tried to get permission to film a zombie movie there.

But the space wasn't empty for long. Like much of the dead commercial real estate of the early aughts, it became a tech campus, a start-up incubator for new ventures. These days it includes a company called HygraTek, which makes coatings for "ice-phobicity," to prevent ice from sticking to aircraft engines, along with some app developers and the thirty-two acres that make up Mcity. Innovation put the smiles back on the lips of the city council members, who rapturously described this new public-private partnership to the press. Their campaign worked: a *Forbes* headline about the project read "A Story of Devastation and Rebirth."

Mcity opened just after Matt and I met. By the time we spent our last afternoon on the hill overlooking its roadways, our conversations were filled with questions about Matt's job search, his interviews, the likelihood of his being hired somewhere we both could live and work. The Ann Arbor landscape seemed already to exist without us, full of cars built to enact human desires, to make even driving ourselves obsolete.

Few places feel so ruined when they're still brand-new. The Mcity sidewalks were immaculate but empty, the patio furniture devoid of life. The bright green highway sign with its reflective lettering held the eye, like a snippet broken off from the whole and out of place, the chunk of four-lane road you might see after an earthquake. The landscape was plastic, flimsy, its flatness an invitation for the chaos of the world to crumble the edges of its highways and dull the yellow of its paint. To invite the deterioration of all the innovation seed money buried in a Michigan field.

Despite challenges to the industry, self-driving cars continue to secure investment. When I last heard from the man who told me he loved the loop, he had gone to work for Cruise Automation, a company that engineers autonomous vehicles that "learn with every mile they drive."

Just a year before he started, in 2018, a woman named Elaine Herzberg was killed by a self-driving car as she wheeled her bike across a four-lane road in Tempe, Arizona. The car was going thirty-nine miles per hour when it hit her, and it didn't appear to slow down before the impact. The autonomous vehicle was a prototype designed by Uber. Originally, it operated with two human employees inside—one to watch the road and take over the controls if necessary, the other to monitor the vehicle's computer system and record data. But according to the National Transportation Safety Board's crash report, Uber had decided one employee could perform both functions. This driver was in the car for backup, but she couldn't take over the controls in time. She was distracted, looking down at her phone when the accident happened. One of the findings in the report was that Uber had cultivated an inadequate safety culture, in part because the company had not created enough mechanisms to address "operators' automation complacency."

When something unexpected materializes and a human driver takes over for an autonomous system, it's called a disengagement. After the crash, it was revealed that in the loose regulatory climate of Arizona, Uber had not been required to share the data on how many times its drivers performed these disengagements.

On the Hacker News forum at Y Combinator, people in the self-driving car business reacted to news of the crash. Many subscribed to the idea that self-driving cars would make fewer errors than people, and therefore keep roads safer. Some of the commenters were horrified, calling Uber's system negligent and pointing out how the start-up ethos of "Move Fast and Break Things" had actually killed someone. Other commenters showed such complete disregard for the victim that I won't reproduce their words here. They treated the world as a video game.

To a non-engineer like myself, the term "disengagement" is perverse. When a human disengages an autonomous system, it means she has to pay attention to her surroundings instead of trusting it all to the car. In this sense, even the term "disengagement" is from the perspective of the vehicle. But riding in self-driving cars, getting used to their autonomy, and letting go of human control are all actions with the potential to reduce our awareness of our environment. Herzberg's death happened because both the driver of the car and the company behind it were deeply disengaged from their surroundings. The backup driver was watching TV, tuning out her job. And Uber was operating in Tempe with cars whose automated systems were not adequately designed to handle one of the most ordinary aspects of city life—jaywalking pedestrians.

Elaine Herzberg was creative. In her free time, she made drawings and poems. At forty-nine, she'd been through hard times, cultivated a wicked sense of humor, had grandchildren and a daughter, who wrote that her mother was generous to her community and would give those in need the shirt off her back. But to the car she was an "edge case"—hard to classify. In the few seconds before impact, the car recognized her first as a vehicle, then as an unknown object, then as a bike. Never as a human.

When Matt was still in pain days after his accident, I made him go back to the hospital. There, they injected his veins with contrast and ran CT scans to check for internal bleeding. I was and still am haunted by a video from high school drivers' ed about a couple who get into a crash. She's driving, he's reading the map. They collide with a lumber truck, and the man stays in the ICU in a coma. The woman goes home, lies on the couch, and soon the

camera zooms in on her abdomen, switching to an eighties anima-
tion of blood cells like red Cheerios escaping from her ruptured
spleen. The absence of a visible injury ends up killing her. I don't
know why the panicked regions of my memory can reproduce this
video so clearly. Maybe I've just always distrusted the sham seren-
ity of the open road.

All Matt's imaging came back normal. I met him outside the hospital so we could walk home, watching the blue square of his parka
descend the steps toward me. We crossed a street, then a river. We
got under the covers and slept for what felt like a week. Soon he
was back in the studio, and I was back on a plane. The cars had
gone inside for the winter, he told me, but the flat people were still
there. The weather began to turn cold, and the stalks of grass on
the hill by his studio turned brittle, hissing in the wind from the
north. The rest of the landscape was silent, he said, like a place that
had been vanquished by a conquering army. As if we might still
live in a world where losing a war means fields sowed with salt.

Since the Territory of Michigan was incorporated on stolen land in
1805, the state has consumed approximately half its forests, a third
of its wetlands, and over 99 percent of its native grasslands. The
history of Michigan's habitat loss is closely related to the origins
of its car culture. William Crapo Durant, the founder of General
Motors, got his middle name from his grandfather, a lumber baron
who made a fortune logging Michigan's pines. Ford was also fi-
nanced with lumber money, as was Cadillac. Now there are only
forty-nine acres of old-growth pine left in the Lower Peninsula.
And one less meadow, mown for self-driving cars.

How do you write a ruin? Conservationist Eileen Crist argues that it's
done by "renaming fish 'fisheries,' animals 'livestock,' trees 'timber,' rivers 'freshwater,' mountaintops 'overburden,' and seacoasts
'beachfront,' so as to legitimize conversion, extermination, and com-
modification ventures." The flattening of a coastline into a real estate

beachfront is akin to the flattening of a coyote into a silent goose alarm. But soon it may get harder to tell the difference. Will some people repeat the lie so often they believe it? Two generations from now, or five, will the absence of coyotes be *convincingly* replaced by stenciled cutouts? Will developers emerge from their reverse-Eden frenzy of renaming, only to find they've written themselves into a dead mall the size of the world?

When I was a child, the car was full of flattened earths, whole seat pockets bulging with maps for everywhere my family had ever driven. Taking a vacation, moving houses, going hiking all meant buying a new map. Then there was the process of orientation, of recognizing the world in the straight lines stretched across your lap, reading through coffee stains and crumbs. Maps hid the complexity of landscape so you could find one particular way through it, one highlighted route across the confusing proliferation of choices. I liked to find the oddest street names in the index on the back and trace my finger to their neatly labeled quadrants.

Since the beginning of automobile technology, the landscape and the car have always evolved in tandem. The long straightaways and gentle curves of highways are already friendly to cruise control. But it's hard for city planners to entirely anticipate how the confluence of technologies that create self-driving might interact with roads, and what they might require of them. When drivers rely on a car to brake and accelerate by itself, it's helpful for the landscape to be as predictable as it is on paper, to avoid sharp turns or unexpected roadblocks, to keep wildlife away from major arteries. In one likely scenario, self-driving cars scan their surroundings as they drive, share the data, and turn the world itself into a map. The next autonomous vehicle mimics the first car, mirroring its path through the streets. But we are now in a period of trial and error. I'm old enough to remember when GPS was even faultier than it is today, when it advised people to take a left off the Pacific Highway into the ocean, or located Walmart in a field of rice. One early GPS adopter even went on NPR to tell the story of her in-laws, who lived on a cul-de-sac that had been mistakenly entered into mapping software as a through street between two major roads. All night, cars would turn around in their driveway, until one person who reached the dead end was frustrated enough to set their car on fire.

One of the strangest aspects of navigation software is that the routes chosen by the algorithm can drive sudden influxes of people to isolated places. Google Maps and Waze have already created traffic patterns just by sending thousands of drivers through a small town as an alternate route. In Leonia, New Jersey, the problem created so much gridlock on the narrow streets that residents couldn't get out of their driveways and had to beg rerouted commuters to let them into the line of cars. But Waze's use of crowd-sourced information created the opportunity to disrupt these "shortcuts." Frustrated people in small towns started going on Waze and reporting accidents that weren't there, just to keep people away from their part of town. There's an ingenuity to these parades and construction projects that exist only in navigation software—ghost roadblocks for the sole purpose of routing vehicles another way.

When I last searched for an image of Mcity, I saw that the flat storefronts had been painted to look like businesses in Ann Arbor's downtown. There was the awning of a sports bar, the glassy windows of an independent bookstore. The flat cutouts of people were still there, painted bright white, dressed in lab coats that hung from their wooden frames like capes on Halloween superheroes. Why this twee locality? Were they hoping that this fake city would be mistaken for some proverbial college town? Would the cars eventually learn the difference? What worries me is that Mcity's tech promise might actually help change the world—for the worse. True automation complacency means that if the world is a map read by a machine, you never need to cultivate the intimacy with landscape that comes from wayfinding ability. You don't need to process the distance between two places or commit the journey to memory. Everywhere you are is a backdrop.

✎

"The memory of what is not may be better than the amnesia of what is," landscape artist Robert Smithson writes. "It is the dimension of absence that remains to be found." But how to find a way to that dimension? One spring afternoon, Matt and I were standing on that hill in Ann Arbor after picking up some boxes from his studio. In just a few weeks, we were moving to Providence, where he'd gotten a job at RISD, and I'd been offered teaching in Boston, only forty-five minutes away. We were drunk on the optimism of this development, grinning at each other as we knelt in the chaos of the half-packed studio, going through whole rolls of clear tape. *I won't have a reason to come back here*, I thought, and as this crossed my mind, I felt a sudden tenderness for the lumpy hill where we'd eaten our lunches, an urge to really look at this place, to absorb it, knowing that soon we'd be gone. I paused, and expected the usual shift in perception that comes with listening, how the air reveals the sounds of birds and bugs, the quiet friction of plants and trees. But I heard nothing.

It's odd to try to write into this void, to express the silence of a meadow where there were only two main noises—the road, and my own breath. Where once there might have been a dozen animal cries, there was just one, or none. It frightened me that I had barely noticed, that over the course of my short life, I'd become accustomed to fewer layers of natural sound.

Radio has an apt term for this silence—*dead air*. In broadcasting, dead air means a total malfunction, a going dark of the equipment or the operator falling asleep. Most radio stations have silence sensors, alarms that go off if silence persists for more than a few seconds, like the machines in a hospital that monitor a patient's vital signs. Standing there overlooking Mcity was one of the first times in my life that I heard a kind of ecological silence, a flatness in the aural landscape, an absence that triggered a subtle but persistent unease.

I had been reading Michael McCarthy, a writer and naturalist who calls this kind of absence "the great thinning," meaning the loss of ordinary, common species, not through extinction, but through a drastic reduction in numbers. How was it possible to see only one sparrow in an afternoon, one moth, one carpenter ant? It's obvious to McCarthy, a baby boomer who watched this wildlife loss unfold. "As we come to the end of our time," he writes of his age group, "a different way of categorising us is beginning to manifest itself: we were the generation who, over the long course of our lives, saw the shadow fall across the face of the earth."

This kind of thinning creates a feeling of disquiet, a sense that something is missing, but only if you know that there was once something there at all. Like a dealership where you trade in a car for the new model, dictionaries have become sites of dynamic obsolescence in language—a record of what needs to be cycled in and out of the lexicon to make these reference books relevant and marketable each year. That shiny newness can hold up a mirror to trends in cultural evolution. In 2015, the *Oxford Junior Dictionary* came under fire for dropping a list of words from the living world and increasing the number of words from technology and business. This five-thousand-word reference book, aimed at seven-year-olds, now includes the words "database," "broadband," "committee," and "cope." It no longer includes: "acorn," "allotment," "almond," "ash," "beaver," "beech," "blackberry," "boar," "brook," "cheetah," "clover," "crocus," "dandelion," "doe," "fern," "fungus," "hazel," "heron," "ivy," "kingfisher," "lark," "leopard," "lobster," "magpie," "minnow," "mussel," "newt," "otter," "oyster,"

"panther," "poppy," "porcupine," "raven," "starling," "sycamore,"
"tulip," "vine," "violet," "walnut," "weasel," "willow," or "wren."
Several of these species are endangered, but others are common.
Bivalves like oysters and mussels help to filter toxins from aquatic
ecosystems. Newts can be bioindicators, signaling the health of their
environments. The word "fungus" represents an entire kingdom—
the same taxonomic rank as "plant" and "animal."

Of course, there are other ways to learn these words, but it's harder
to notice what you can't name, and harder still to advocate for it. As
a child of the late eighties and early nineties, I'm not even sure how
much of the shadow I can see. With every generation, the amount
of wildlife decreases, and the understanding of what's "normal"
becomes thinner and thinner. As a species, we become more alone,
but we also become less able to perceive our ecological loneliness.

I'm too young to remember the "moth snowstorms" McCarthy
describes, in which cars were enveloped by thousands of hinged,
white wings. I've never driven through a cloud of insects so thick
I had to stop and wash the windshield, running the squeegee over
a mess of stuck gossamer. It occurs to me that these kills were actually a sign of abundance—that humans are living with a pattern
of wildlife loss that is not less dangerous because it has no visual
symptom. Hitting nothing—having nothing to hit—should trigger alarm bells, but it just feels like smoothness, the perfect curves
of open lanes that car commercials teach us to expect.

Because it can be monetized and invested in, autonomy is loneliness's neoliberal cousin. I don't want to assume that because self-
driving cars are theoretically free from human-driver error, that
because they reduce our responsibility, they will improve the places
of our daily lives and the lives of the beings who share them. There
is a world of implications beyond the narrow lens of human convenience and optimization. Eventually, self-driving cars will be pro-
grammed to recognize every possible "edge case," to absorb which

shapes in the road are acceptable to hit (birds, squirrels, turtles, newts, rabbits) and which should provoke braking or a swerve (humans, deer).

That afternoon, as we stood in the dead quiet overlooking the fake self-driving city, we could imagine a future where the last man on Earth summons an autonomous car from the ruins of a Detroit auto show. The car knows each turn of the road, each shape of an animal that might cross its path, though the landscape will be almost empty. This pattern recognition will be a form of ecological memory. Like a bird watcher's list, if the birds were remembered only as obstacles, as varying nonhuman shapes with limited potential to fuck up a car.

Birds seen 6ª July 1989 in Cornwall Hollow: in 2hr walk.

Flicker
Yellow throat
Yellow warbler
Chestnut-sided warbler

Chipping sparrow

Song sparrow
Phoebe
Cedar Waxwing

Crow
Red-wing blackbird

Bluebird

Cardinal

Robin
Catbird
House wren

Vireo
Goldfinch
Kinglet

Kingbird
Baltimore Oriole
Least flycatcher

Tree Swallows
Bank Swallow
Cliff swallow
Savannah Sparrow

Earlier in June/July also:

Great-Horned Owl
Red-tail Hawk
Turkey Buzzard
Turkey
Grouse
Pileated Woodpecker
Killdeer
Green heron
Scarlet Tanager
Indigo bunting
Redstart
Ruffed Grouse
Chestnut-sided Towhee
~~Prothonotary warbler~~
Rose-breasted Grossbeak
Black + white warbler
blue-wing warbler
White-breasted nuthatch
Jay
Woodpecker (hairy)

4

Cancerine

There is a photo my father must have taken, of me as a child, emerging from ankle-deep muck, the scion of a prehistoric arthropod clasped in my fist by the lip of its shell. I would often land these horseshoe crabs from out of the marsh and then return them, at his orders, lingering until the dazed animals once again began to move.

To land a species means to take it to shore, to bring an animal across the primeval transition zone where gills once became lungs. Today, landings are carried out by fisheries and measured in pounds and value of catch. A landed creature is usually a dead one, but there are exceptions. Humans land horseshoe crabs, harvest their immune cells for biomedical testing, and then return them to the ocean alive, minus a prescribed amount of their beluga-blue blood.

Limulus polyphemus is the official name for the Atlantic horseshoe crab. Like tardigrades, horseshoe crabs and their ancestors have been on Earth longer than dinosaurs. They've lived through all five mass extinctions, surviving on this planet for some 445 to 475 million years. Though everyone calls them crabs, they're actually a different kind of arthropod—more closely related to scorpions and spiders. Part of my early fascination with *limulus* came from the way they carry other species, becoming itinerant microcosms of aquatic invertebrate life. Over time, mature horseshoe crabs accumulate small cities of marine creatures on their shells, including colonies of bacteria, snails, worms, slipper shells, barnacles, sponges, fringed ghost anemones, and the quick, pink tentacles of sea strawberries. Naturalist Dave Grant writes that some members of this "moving menagerie" rely on the horseshoe crab to hitch a ride out of the silt. Other species simply settle on the shells of these crabs as they move across the bottom of the sea, making the horseshoe crab a "living fossil" with the contents of a tide pool on its back. They're comfortable in the depths of Atlantic bays, but they can survive temporarily in air. When they come up on land to mate, they have book gills whose folded, page-like membranes can keep them alive out of the water for as long as the book stays damp.

I wish I could say that *limulus* translates to "liminal," appropriate for an animal that troubles the threshold between the terrestrial and watery worlds. In fact, the first part of the name means "askance," or "oblique," which is less interesting than *Polyphemus*, the Cyclops of the *Odyssey*, who is literally robbed blind in the myth, stabbed in his one eye by Odysseus, who sneaks into his cave by hiding his men under the pelts of a stolen flock. This species of arthropod got its name because it was initially thought to have only one eye, though the naming is more appropriate when you consider *Limulus polyphemus*'s bizarre relationship with humans—whose theft of horseshoe crabs has made us perennial wolves in sheep's clothing.

In the story, when Polyphemus is left alone, abandoned and injured, he asks his father, Poseidon, to curse Odysseus. As he's left to die, Polyphemus (ancient, other, monster, child of a god) can't stand the idea that Odysseus's survival will grant the man any kind of automatic moral victory. At the very least, the Cyclops begs the

sea god, let Odysseus's return be lonely rather than heroic—a pun-
ishment to make homecoming bittersweet. Though his sight has
been devastated, the Cyclops gets the last word, troubling the finality of just who is surviving whom. In Emily Wilson's translation,
Polyphemus cries to the stars

> Grant that Odysseus, the city-sacker,
> will never go back home. Or if it is
> fated that he will see his family,
> then let him get there late and with no honor,
> in pain and lacking ships, and having caused
> the death of all his men, and let him find
> more trouble in his own house.

My father read me the *Odyssey* while recovering from radiation
treatment. We'd sit outside, in chairs facing the marsh, as his voice
rose and fell like the swallows that nested under the raised slats of
a neighbor's deck. In summer, the memory of him is strongest,
returning not in details but in a kind of pressure on my conscious-
ness, the way liquid in a barometer signals a storm.

A bubble of accumulated images: We are walking across a marsh at
low tide, the marks of deep mud creeping up our shins. We are in
a field of flattened grasses, a clearing where deer have slept within
the wall of tawny reeds. We're beneath the branches of dead saplings, their roots plunged in brackish water, a ghost forest at the
edge of the tide.

What still hovers is his kindness: I, the child, found a horseshoe
crab one day, and wanted to open its leg to see if the blood was
really blue. And my father appeared and said, "Animals don't like
to be poked with sticks!"

As usual, the story shifts. The knowledge of my father's absence blooms here as it does everywhere—even, eventually, in dreams. When I remember he's dead, it means I'm waking, about to blink my way into another morning's chill.

～

Despite their Cyclopean name, horseshoe crabs have ten eyes, remarkable ones, that allow them to see as well by moonlight as they do under the noon sun. Their biggest eyes, the lateral ones, have light receptors that are easy to notice, even without a microscope—they look like tiny black pinpricks in the silvery mirror of their eyes. Or like the pebbled shadows of a reflector on the back of a bike. A strong circadian rhythm adjusts these receptors to become a million times more photosensitive at night, and they have been known to preserve this inner clock even when cloistered in a darkened tank.

As creatures from the tidal zone, theirs is a world of rhythms not easily forgotten or undone—of waves, of seasons, of migrations, of the moon, of the piling up of dunes and their erosion back into the sea. Their oldest ancestors were alive at moments when inland oceans dried up and sea levels rose over islands—when the world warmed and there were vast changes in the salinity and temperature of the tides. As Rachel Carson writes in *The Rocky Coast*, "To understand the shore, it is not enough to catalogue its life. Understanding comes only when, standing on a beach, we can sense the long rhythms of earth and sea that sculptured its forms and produced the rock and sand of which it is composed; when we can sense with the eye and ear of the mind the surge of life beating always at its shores—blindly, inexorably pressing for a foothold."

Humans still don't really know how the world looks to a horseshoe crab, or all the reasons their eyes evolved to see. Vision researcher Robert Barlow had a breakthrough when he discovered that males use their sight to find mates along the beach. Though some suspect it, we're not sure if they return to nest where they hatched, and what role vision might play in the doings of their underwater world.

These gaps create significant mystery. Carson continues: "To understand the life of the shore, it is not enough to pick up an empty shell and say 'This is a murex' or 'That is an angel wing.' True understanding demands intuitive comprehension of the whole life of the creature that once inhabited this empty shell: how it survived amid surf and storms, what were its enemies, how it found food and reproduced its kind, what were its relations."

The road to the house where my father died runs through a marsh, along a causeway between inlets ringed with spartina and phragmites. During early-morning tides, the light comes slatted through the reeds and gilds the scum on the water into an oily, golden brew. When the marsh floods, the salt veers across the yellow line into the brackish ponds on the other side of the road. These salt migrations have a name—they are called king tides, triggered by the moon at the apex of its gravitational pull on the water.

Horseshoe crabs arrive with the moon, too. The light receptors along their bodies can sense when the moonlight changes and shifts, orienting their circadian rhythms to the actual clock of dawn and dusk. In late spring and summer, at the full and new moons when the tides are highest, these arthropods come up on the beaches to spawn along the coast of New England. Though their movements are associated with the cycles of the moon, horseshoe crabs likely navigate by the slope of the beach and the currents, rather than by moonlight itself. They sometimes gather on tidal flats just off the beach and wait for the tide to rise, preferring the moment when the water is highest.

Other creatures wait for them. Deborah Cramer has written about the vital connections between bird populations and *limulus*, especially in Delaware Bay, where the beaches are massive breeding sites for the crabs, whose abundance and predictable timing have nourished many migrations of red knots. They feed on *limulus* eggs on their way north to the Arctic. The eggs are also food for fish, American eels, and sea turtles, making horseshoe crabs a keystone species, an essential part of other animals' survival strategies.

It's impossible to think about the prospect or scope of human extremotolerance without considering the other animals we've used to bolster our own resilience. Horseshoe crabs are a prime example—over the last 150 years, humans have relied on them in moments of scarcity and crisis, when our tolerance for changing resources was nearing its limits. The first example of extreme harvesting of *limulus* began in the mid-nineteenth century, when farmers began to use them in significant numbers as fertilizer for their fields.

This systematic use of horseshoe crabs was born out of desperation. By the first half of the nineteenth century, landowners had depleted Delaware's soil, pushing it to exhaustion through plantation-economy practices of over-farming cash crops. Many landlords used enslaved labor to work the fields, or divided their holdings between sharecroppers, requiring their impoverished tenants to grow mostly corn. In places, crop yields became so poor that tenant farmers resorted to stripping the bark off oak trees and selling it to tanners to eke out a living, an unexpected consequence of soil exhaustion that decimated Delaware's black oaks. At the time, one agricultural reformer wrote: "Under such a system, destruction of the soil is rapid and certain."

Something, officials realized, had to be done about the dirt. At first, they tried importing seabird guano all the way from Peru and excavating marl, a clayey rock containing the lime of crushed seashells. But importing guano was impractical, and marl was heavy to transport. So they turned to a local fertilizer, which, like many of the extractive "solutions" applied by the colonists, had its origins in sustainable, Indigenous practices.

In the early 1600s, Samuel de Champlain, the quote-unquote "Father of New France," observed that the Indigenous people who planted corn along the Maine coast would take dead horseshoe crabs and bury them in the corn mounds to increase the crop. By the mid-1800s, the settlers in Delaware had begun to do something similar, using horseshoe crabs as fertilizer. Initially, the settlers harvested crabs in much the same way I plucked them out of the mud as a child. People would walk out into the tidal flats and marshes and pick them up by their shells. And at first, the horseshoe crabs were abundant enough to provide nutrients for the soil.

But by 1870, crab fertilizer had caught on. Part of the harvesting process included drying the crabs that had been pulled from the tidal flats, and in the Delaware public archives, you can see photos of these stacks of dying and dead *limulus* rising out of the sand. The sepia tint makes the carnage look gentler and yet somehow more strange—great curving masses along the shoreline that slowly register as thousands of individual shells. In one summer of that decade, over four million horseshoe crabs were collected. Four million. An ocean of death edging the beach, stinking in the summer heat. This ancient species of arthropod was piled along boardwalks like a fieldstone wall, but with a sinister glossiness, a hint of the living creatures decaying within their nitrogen-rich shells. Horse-drawn wagonloads of crabs waited outside the factories to be ground down, a bounty taller than a man.

The process was quickly optimized. People captured crabs in their breeding grounds in structures called "pounds" and stacked them to desiccate, then carted them to a factory, where they were run through giant blenders and turned into powder. This powder was sold as a fertilizer and spread over fields across the Northeast. The product was christened Cancerine.

⤙

A cancer means a crab, until it suddenly doesn't. When, exactly, does an animal become a backdrop for human concerns? Is it possible to pinpoint the moment an ecosystem becomes a stage set in a vast passion play among people, and if so, can this anthropocentrism be reversed?

It would be easy to say that when an animal enters the market, it stops being an animal and becomes a commodity, and that it remains a commodity for as long as it exists and has salable value. But I resist the reductive cynicism of that sentence. As theorist Timothy Morton writes in *Dark Ecology*, "Capitalist economics is also an anthropocentric practice that has no easy way to factor in the very things that ecological thought and politics require: nonhuman beings and unfamiliar timescales." To reframe the harvest of horseshoe crabs from an ecological perspective is to notice the way humans are not just observers of *limulus*, not just bystanders or researchers, but the opposite—we are deeply enmeshed in a long interspecies cycle of boom-and-bust.

These crabs are resilient animals—they've proven their resilience by lasting through the geological changes of the past four hundred million years. By contrast, humans and their ancestors have overlapped with these creatures for only a few million years. For at least fifty of those years, humans pulled more than a million individual horseshoe crabs from the sea annually, and sometimes as many as four million. In less than one human lifetime, in an eyeblink, people have wiped out at minimum fifty to one hundred million crabs in the Delaware Bay area alone. That's a punishing clash of time scales.

The year I was born, my father turned sixty, and my mother turned forty-two. When I return now to the marshlands of my child-hood, it is usually to visit her. Year-round, she lives in the house she shares with his memory, watching the water come and go over the same tidal flats. We often walk west as the sun is going down, toward the oceanfront, where the picture windows of the wealthy reflect the glow back out to sea. We pause at a small pier where you have to watch your step—gulls drop mollusk shells from on high, cracking them open to reveal the meat. Here, where it's easy to connect to the animal world, the human story is harder.

This is Guilford, Connecticut—an old New England town where the veil of quaintness hangs heavy. Despite the amnesia of every-day use, the place-names on this shoreline carry a history that is far from casual. Bloody Cove, Old Sachems Head Road, Indian Road, Arrowhead Drive. As a child, I was told that the name "Sachem's Head" came from a conflict between the Mohegan and the Pequot, but if you dig deeper, that's not actually the whole story. An English captain called Richard Davenport named this spit of land in 1637, when he wrote a letter to his superiors describing how he was part of a raiding party who killed their Pequot captives here. Scholar and Guilford resident Hazel Carby has recently pointed out that websites about the town have "nothing to say about a letter . . . describing his interrogation of Pequot prisoners whom 'we put to death that night and called the place Sacheme head.'" By way of explanation, Davenport notes in the margin of his account that one of the captives "was a Sachem."

By 1897, though, the story of the name had shifted. In *A History of the Plantation of Menunkatuck and of the Original Town of Guilford, Connecticut*, based on the accounts of Ralph Dunning Smyth (and written and complied by his grandson Bernard Christian Steiner), Captain Davenport isn't mentioned, and neither is his role as a representative of the colonial forces, claiming credit for a military advance. Instead, the presence of the white settlers in the raiding party has been reduced to "a few of the Connecticut soldiers," none of whom are named. Steiner and Smyth recast the conflict as one between the fleeing Pequots and the Mohegan Sachem Uncas, who had allied himself with the British in the face of mass killings. Smyth goes out of his way to say that Menunkatuck (Guilford) had not yet been settled, and names Uncas as the executioner of the Pequot sachem: "Uncas himself," Smyth writes, "is said to have shot him with an arrow."

In her book *Firsting and Lasting*, Ojibwe historian Jean O'Brien points out that colonial histories also locate Guilford as home to New England's oldest stone house, built in 1639 (a date the town's websites still use). These histories calculate where to emphasize settler presence—when it comes to buildings, the dates go back as far as possible, but when it comes to violence, the English presence is postdated and minimized. O'Brien writes that in these subtler ways, "stories about the land and the events that transpired in particular places performed the cultural work of seizing Indian homelands."

On these quiet streets, you can chart a whole arc of suppressed violence: from the massacres of the 1600s to the crises of the ecological future. At the tip of the cove, where the very wealthiest live, I can just make out the home of the biotech magnate who built himself a replica of Stonehenge at the edge of the water. He asked his design team to ensure it would last ten thousand years, because, as he told a reporter, "ten thousand years is on the same order of magnitude as recorded history." Advised that the stones would likely be underwater in a hundred years, he was "O.K. with that." Never mind sea level rise—the standing stones will survive, aligned to the celestial patterns of his children's birthdays. To me, these hunks of Norwegian granite represent seven hundred tons of "environmental load displacement"—the idea that the consumers who use the most resources are often those who bear the least impact from their extraction. When his Stonehenge is underwater, how many other people will have had their towns and monuments and traces washed away? He calls the replica, unironically, The Circle of Life.

~

The overharvesting of *limulus* for fertilizer tapered off in the early twentieth century, and by 1960, the market had all but disappeared. The beachfronts were becoming lucrative coastal real estate, and local homeowners were complaining that the horseshoe crab industry reeked. *Limulus* had been so depleted by this point that fishermen were putting in a great deal of effort and time for little catch. Besides, the product wasn't so profitable anymore—there were synthetic alternatives for Cancerine.

The man who ultimately made the pulverizing of horseshoe crabs obsolete was named Fritz Haber, and he was a German chemist who first became famous for synthesizing the nutrients necessary to ameliorate depleted soil. Nitrogen, he discovered, could be harvested from the air. By the mid 1900s, Haber's innovation was successful on a commercial scale, alleviating soil exhaustion and famine. Haber won the Nobel Prize in Chemistry. His invention allowed the system of extractive farming to continue, so that it no longer meant the end of the soil's fertility. With synthetic fertilizer, nitrogen could be spread across the earth in amounts far greater than the original soil concentrations.

But along with discovering synthetic fertilizer, Haber is known as the father of chemical warfare. In 1915, the man who was indirectly responsible for slowing the immediate decline of *limulus* led a team of scientists to develop and deploy poison gas in the trenches of the First World War. He oversaw several of these deployments himself on the German front lines, including the first gas attack at Ypres, which killed upward of five thousand troops. One surviving Canadian sergeant would later call the effects of chlorine gas "an equivalent death to drowning only on dry land," a phrase that is eerily reminiscent of what happens when a horseshoe crab's book gills are kept in air too long. Later in life, Haber's alchemical yearnings met their limit. He tried, without success, to pay for German war reparations by developing a process that could harvest minute amounts of gold from ocean water.

Late one night, I stumble on a shitty article in a magazine called *Corporate Connecticut* that's titled "Crab Blood Is Gold (or Why a Living Fossil May Save Your Life)."

These days, a quart of American horseshoe crab blood sells for about fifteen thousand dollars. Up and down the Atlantic coast, biomedical companies harvest this blue fluid for medical testing because it has the property of alerting us to even tiny amounts of gram-negative bacteria, a dangerous and common contaminant in medical products. If they get into the bloodstream, these bacteria can release endotoxins that cause lethally high fevers. As William Sargent writes in his book *Crab Wars*, endotoxins are often called pyrogens, or "burning bodies," because of how dangerously they can make a fever rise. Every batch of intravenous drugs—vaccines, chemotherapy medications, dyes for imaging, vitamins, anything that comes out of a drip or is implanted in a human—must be proven safe before it can be sold. Before 1970, batches of vaccines, intravenous drugs, and other medical formulas were simply tested on rabbits to ensure safety. To make their products on an industrial scale, pharmaceutical companies had to have huge numbers of live rabbits on hand. If you shot up a batch of them with vaccine and they spiked fevers, you knew your product was contaminated. This was called the rabbit pyrogen test.

Horseshoe crab blood became so valuable because it offers a simpler and more sensitive test. *Limulus polyphemus* has an immune system that may well be one of the oldest in the world. When a horse-shoe crab is infected with harmful bacteria, amebocytes (immune cells) in its blood release clotting proteins around the infection, like human platelets do around a wound. In the lab, when these components of horseshoe blood are mixed with a contaminated substance, the clotting is instantly visible as blue film in a test tube—you don't have to wait for hours or speculate on the warmth of a terrified rabbit.

The *Limulus* Amebocyte Lysate (LAL) test is still the gold standard. And lately, we've needed horseshoe crabs more than ever. In 2020, American drug companies used LAL to test billions of doses of COVID-19 vaccine. This fact is even more striking when you consider that a synthetic alternative to lysate is now available. Though the synthetic version would be cheaper in the long run, the current guidelines make it cumbersome to use. Vaccine makers still have to carry an extra burden of proof if they want the FDA to approve their product based on testing with the synthetic chemical rather than with horseshoe crab blood. European authorities have accepted that the synthetic can be treated as an equivalent, and the US was on the verge of taking the same step, but despite pressure from conservationist groups, the COVID-19 pandemic placed such scrutiny on vaccines and vaccine safety that regulatory groups in America pushed back their widespread acceptance of the alternative test. As Ryan Phelan, a biomedical nonprofit director, told the *New York Times*: "It is crazy making that we are going to rely on a wild animal extract during a global pandemic."

She has a point. But when you know the history of human reliance on horseshoe crabs, it's not surprising that we turned to them once again. Over the last century, we've intertwined both our resilience and our immunity with theirs. Over the last half century, when humans have extracted wildlife and created habitat loss, when we've released new zoonoses into circulation among global populations, we've turned to horseshoe crabs to manufacture safe treatments. As we bolster our immunity to COVID through the use of vaccines, it's because horseshoe crabs have been our poison testers. We can talk about saving the horseshoe crab, and scientists like the late Carl Shuster have done important work to preserve their habitat. But it's equally important to recognize that it's not just about whether biomedical companies, bait fishermen, and regulators want to offer Atlantic horseshoe crabs some clemency. The illusion of human control masks the question of whether clemency is even ours to offer—when humans have been in dire straits, over and over again, *Limulus polyphemus* has rescued us.

Here's a question I can ask only in retrospect. When my father taught me horseshoe anatomy, when he showed me their eyes and told me that their tails are called telsons, when he explained the myth of Polyphemus's blindness, when he walked me through the differences between the iron in our blood and the copper in theirs, did he know the cancer treatments transfused into him had been vetted by an unclotted extract drawn from that same blood?

On our walks through the marshlands, we didn't talk that much about his illness. It felt sometimes like he'd decided to resolve his relationship to being sick, at least in front of me. As if a person could compartmentalize cancer the way you bracket a thought. If I asked him about it, he'd say his disease was well managed—the drugs made the cancer grow so slowly that old age would likely kill him first.

When I was thirteen, he went to a new oncologist to ask for a second opinion. The doctor told him he had six months to live. I didn't know, at the time, about this new prognosis. But I saw how his eyes changed when he looked at me. There was a sudden weight to his gentleness, a raw shadow at the edge of the frame. As a month passed, and then another, the disease went on changing, imperceptibly, in the depths of his body. A few cells continued their slow progression of aberrance. In the end, neither prognosis was right. The cancer would kill him. But it would take years, not months.

～

Though they are not extremotolerant, horseshoe crabs are an adaptable species that has often been valorized for the ability to bounce back from both prehistoric challenges and human harvesting. One of the few general-audience books on horseshoe crabs is subtitled *Biography of a Survivor*. I've seen them called "old soldier crabs," too. This kind of phrasing interests me because I sense in it that same moral superiority associated with rugged individualism, with ideas of undergoing pain and living to tell the tale. Why this projection of toughness onto the mysterious life of an arthropod? I wonder if insisting on their resilience makes humans feel better about the harm. As if horseshoe crabs were a comrade species, a companion in ecological loneliness, when some people and corporations damage the landscapes we all need to survive. But besides the usual charge of anthropomorphizing a crab, doesn't valorizing the strength of these creatures hide our guilt at needing so much from them? Their namesake, Polyphemus, certainly doesn't buy Odysseus's toughness when he curses the cruelty of his city-sacking ways. Instead, the Cyclops calls for the human to be the sole survivor of all his men, a position without honor. In old stories like this one, the sea god's curse is the one that holds.

If they carry out their full life cycle, horseshoe crabs don't die alone. By the end of their time, they resemble gardens of seaweed and shells, snails attached to their undersides, barnacles encroaching on their eyes. Eventually their backs are so crowded with other creatures that they become sluggish with the drag. The plants and animals grow over their eyes, like a thicket over a ruin, and they go blind. It's not a soldier's death in battle but the end of a gradual symbiosis, a slow transition to the seafloor they resemble. But when crabs enter a biomedical facility for their blood to be harvested, one of the first things technicians do is scrub everything off their shells.

In the bleeding process, companies can harvest up to 30 percent of a crab's blood, and an estimated 10 to 30 percent of individuals die. But there are holes in this data. That figure doesn't include what really happens when they're returned to the water. Many are stressed by extreme temperatures in transit. Many are also noticeably affected after being put back in their habitat—in one study, when the horseshoe crabs were observed for two weeks after their blood was harvested, they walked slower, were less active in feeding, and females were lethargic, with some failing to spawn at all. Nevertheless, the companies that bleed horseshoe crabs have been favorably regarded by regulators, scientists, and some conservationists. Compared with other fisheries, even a 30 percent mortality rate is theoretically considered low enough to continue sustainably harvesting the species. And besides, the biomedical industry is invested in keeping the horseshoe crab population alive so it can profit from their blood. The prevailing logic seems to be that since many animals are mixed up in human industries one way or another, it's best for a creature to be needed by an industry that places a high value on that animal and doesn't always have to kill it. By extension, this argument goes, we'd better keep using horseshoe crab blood, because if we don't, *limulus* will lose the protection its market value affords. Obviously, this pragmatism is a terrible paradox—biased to favor the money.

After Cancerine became obsolete, there was a brief period when horseshoe crab populations rebounded, and without the harvest, it is possible that their abundance could return. But in the late seventies, alongside the discovery and use of lysate, the crabs began to compensate for the human depletion of another natural resource. Though the soil had regained its fertility, fisheries were collapsing. Many of the trawlers along the Atlantic coast were rigged to catch cod or flounder. But when these stocks were exhausted, the fisher-men needed another catch to preserve their livelihoods. Many turned to catching eel and whelk, which can be lucrative, espe-cially in international markets. The main bait for these catches is egg-laden female horseshoe crabs. In 1999, 1.4 million horseshoe crabs were landed for bait in Virginia alone, putting the number of dead crabs right back at fertilizer-harvest levels. Since then, a robust bait fishery has continued. Despite the implementing of a coast-wide quota for both biomedical and bait landings, there is no way to police the entire shore. Now eel and horseshoe populations are both strained.

"Where is memory?" asks Deborah Cramer. "The nineteenth-century cycle of massive extraction and decimation repeated itself as rising demand for eel and whelk depleted horseshoe crabs once again. . . . We look back, askance, at market gunners who killed thousands of shorebirds and at fishermen who turned millions of horseshoe crabs into fertilizer, but one day our children may ask how we, with more awareness, took one diminished species as bait to catch other species, themselves diminished."

Over the last ten years, horseshoe crab numbers in Long Island Sound have declined, according to the most recent data from the Atlantic State Marine Fisheries Commission. The "stock status" in Connecticut is now rated "poor." At least among the marshes and beachheads of my childhood, horseshoe resilience is waning.

On a shelf in the kitchen of my parents' house, there was a book mysteriously titled *How We Die*. I never let on that I noticed it, and I don't remember either of my parents taking it off the bookcase. It hovered there, a two-inch-thick spine, sitting over my father's shoul-der during meals. Years later, I would pick it up and read, in a chap-ter called "The Malevolence of Cancer," that "with the optimism born of therapeutic successes came a determined cockiness that sometimes goes beyond reason; it finds expression in the philosophy that treatment must be pursued until futility can be proven." Basically, when there are many treatments for a problem, it's easy to be swayed into thinking that the cure is just around the bend, that the complexity of a disease will relent with just one more medical innovation. This lucid explanation comes from a doctor. From the patient's perspective, there are no limits to treatment, except, as Anne Boyer puts it, "the capacity to exhaust oneself to discover a possibility's end." When someone is suffering, resilience can be a tall order, an inhumane demand. My father had a chemotherapy appointment scheduled for the day before he died. But he did not become, in the common parlance of the American Cancer Society, what is called a survivor. Instead, I was left to understand how to relate to the landscape where I had survived him.

My father did not believe that anyone could own a beach. Or a marsh, for that matter. When he came to the US from London, he never shook his belief in public access, footpaths, rights of way across fields. Together we skirted the edges of suburban Connecticut lawns, sloshed through creeks, searched for birds and nests, because, as he told me, nothing below the tide line was private. If anyone asked, I was to say that we'd paddled there in our rowboat. The neighbors were often living elsewhere through whole seasons—golden October sand, we felt, was wasted on them anyway.

Look, he'd say, and there on the sand, the half-translucent wing of a stranded monarch butterfly, the iridescence of a mermaid's toenail shell. In the world of these verges, the sea was an endless reinvention and he was alive to everything that washed ashore. The feeling of those hours is liquid to me—the sense that time was running both away and toward me, between the age of the water molecules and the incoming tide, the filtering currents moving through the grasses, where in fifteen minutes you could touch an eon and let it slip through your fingers.

By all accounts, my father was a trespasser, but he wouldn't have seen it that way. Only in retrospect did I realize how brazen this was, how contingent on the familiarity of our faces—to make a world out of going to the water whenever you wanted, of borrowing, without asking, a neighbor's access to their sea. As the water rises, it submerges our old paths through spartina, our forts of driftwood and reeds. And I am not a child anymore, scrambling behind a mild-mannered man in a corduroy shirt as we follow the coast for hours, shielding each other from inhospitable eyes. The door to this world shut with his death: I haven't wanted to trespass alone.

Last time I walked to the shore, the sky was low-lit, pebbled in the afternoon with a texture of yellow jet trails. Clouds refracted back over the horizon like floating mirages of islands. I like how you can see the bones of wildness better in the cold, the foam blowing, the glint of granite, a hawk diving into a field. At the bluest hour the marshes held their shadows close: tawny spartina dimmed gray with mud. I could smell it—not a salt tang but something sharper and more fetid, seaweed and silt and decay. It's a cold place if you stay through the winter.

"Instead of a vigil—a flight," the poet Adam Zagajewski writes. "Travel instead of remembrance." Before I moved away, I used to examine the mussels gulls had cracked open on the stones of our seawall. I used to watch for wild turkeys in the morning, for the coyotes who followed the deer. I could hum a periwinkle out of its shell or name a bird by its feather. It's hard to stay with the count of names and their wing shapes—house sparrow, little egret, great blue heron. Each one was a gap my father closed between my child's finger pointing skyward and the correct name of a bird. I can't see a tern without thinking of him. My embarrassment was acute when he imitated the raucous squawk of a black-capped night heron in front of my second-grade class, but I've never forgotten its sound. Though I love these remnants, for a long time it was easier to travel, to be somewhere a little less familiar, somewhere that

chafed less against my particular knowledge of loss. To lose someone is to be exiled from the landscape of their knowledge—to be
reminded of all the things you didn't know or didn't ask. How did
he understand the interactions of creatures through their naming?
Now when I try to close the gap myself, I'm left with shadows of
birds' wings and the syllables that sometimes don't come until hours
later, if they come at all. When I'm lucky, the wing shapes pull
names from deep in my memory, like a language I haven't used.

The truth is, a living landscape can never be a monument. The beach
cottages of my childhood have become McMansions, and in places,
you can barely glimpse the sea between the houses. Floodlights
confuse migrating birds, and construction noise sometimes scares
off nesting ospreys. One summer, the lot next door was a vacation
rental, a party spot for New Yorkers who didn't want to go to the
Hamptons. For a while, after the real estate crash of 2008 and hur-
ricanes Sandy and Irene, houses on the street stood empty, waiting
for unwilling buyers. Now the place is busier than ever, though the
water continues to rise.

When I first brought Matt back to visit this place, I saw through
his fresh eyes how much the street had changed. On the oceanfront side of the road, seawalls have replaced beaches, and only a
thin strip of sand emerges at low tide. Many of the homes have hur-
ricane shutters—blast doors that can close when storm surge pum-
mels the second floor. But there's still nowhere else for the water to
go. Even on sunny days, the puddles don't drain. This summer, the
town has decided to tear up the existing road and raise it. Dirt will
be trucked in to elevate and regrade, so that when the road floods,
half the street doesn't become an island, cut off during king tides.
Close to the water, the pink granite of my childhood is still there,
but the tide line has risen, and tiny microplants have turned the
rocks slick and dark. On the wall at the end of the lawn, the air is

heavy with the smell of marsh. I have to avoid catching an ankle in the holes behind the seawall where water crests the top and leaches down, eroding the dirt behind it.

It may be that horseshoe crabs have also declined in Long Island Sound because rising sea and protective building methods have eaten up the places where they once spawned. As I tried to wrap my mind around these changes, I spoke with biologist Jennifer Mattei, who studies the Long Island Sound population. She founded Project Limulus, a community science group that tags and surveys horseshoe crabs during the summer full moons. During our conversation, Mattei told me that as the waters have risen and eaten up the beaches, she's seen *limulus* pairs trying to mate on the lawns of manicured homes—forced to trespass by the changing of the shoreline. When I asked her about the long-term status of these animals, she brought up the concept of "functional extinction"—a term for what happens when a species can no longer perform their role in an ecosystem because they aren't numerous enough. Horseshoe crabs still swim in the shallows, they're still present in this environment, but their abundance is gone. They can't sustain all the other creatures they used to feed.

In early summer, on the eve of the strawberry moon, I drive to Guilford to survey some horseshoe crabs as they're spawning. Though the weather service predicted thunderstorms, some angle of a front has shifted—the moon appears between clouds, ringed by a pale circle of vapor. Wild rugosa roses line the parking spaces. It's a small beach—more of a boat launch, really. An entrance to a huge network of marshes opens at the back of the cove, where kayakers sometimes get trapped by the incoming tide as it pours through the channel. But the water in the bay is sheltered, and the sloped sand is soft. It's early, twenty minutes before the official high-tide mark, but already I can see a pair of horseshoe crabs in the shallows, a smaller male riding on the back of a female as they coast away from my shadow. This close to the marsh, the gnats gather around my headlamp, making me feel like a human porch light.

I'm here to meet Deanna Broderick, who has been surveying horse-shoe crabs for seven years. At the full and new moons, she comes down to this beach, sometimes with her daughter and grand-daughter. Tonight her husband is here to help mark down the data she collects. In waders and a *Project Limulus* T-shirt, she shuffles through the shallows, sometimes recognizing a crab from a previous survey. There's a dead one who washed up that morning, and a female who's a regular, with a gash over her eye. Deanna takes me down to the tide line to show me how they measure and tag the crabs, how a small white disk can anchor to the carapace, where it won't drag in the sand.

Deanna began to do community science work for Project Limulus through the local Audubon Society. She picked this specific beach to survey because she knows it's a notorious site for people who collect and sell horseshoe crabs. There's one man in particular who comes down here whom Deanna refers to as the harvester. Data she helped collect has already been published, but she keeps up the surveys and the tagging, mostly to engage the public and to discourage people from overfishing. "I wanted to do this beach to let the harvesters know we're paying attention," she says. As I watch, the crab she tagged slips back out into the cove, the white circle of his marker fading like an underwater moon.

Down at the most sheltered corner, where a small breakwater has collected soft, silty sand, we find a few more spawning crabs. One of the young males sidles up to Deanna, and she laughs. "That's my foot, buddy." But for her, the numbers are lacking. "Usually this part is crazy—an eightsome, a threesome," she says. "I'm wondering if the harvester has been here."

Thanks to her presence, the neighbors have become more aware of the people who take horseshoe crabs, whether they're operating legally or not. By proxy, they've been caught up, made aware of the drama of extraction, more than I ever was as a kid. Recently, the regulations on horseshoe crab fishing have tightened, but it's nearly impossible to enforce them on these small beaches at night. The neighbors usually tell Deanna if the harvester has come.

This kind of public interest in the world of the horseshoe crab is no small feat. Though she'll jokingly greet horseshoe crabs with "Hey, cutie!," she realizes other people take a little longer to warm up. Her granddaughter, who is eleven, has been surveying with her since she was three years old. Deanna tells me that at first, her granddaughter didn't want to touch the horseshoe crabs who were flipped by waves, but now she does.

By day, Deanna's a dental hygienist. But she tells me she's always been interested in community science, working with local bird sanctuaries, including one for the purple martin, an endangered and iridescent swallow. As I watch, she runs her finger along a female crab's shell where she's buried herself in the sand, to see if she's wearing a tag. There's something moving in Deanna's quick, habitual gestures. This kind of noticing is normal for her—she's following the daily upticks and downturns of this population with unselfconscious care.

Because, as she well knows, the days around the full moon are prime time for harvesting, too. After the survey, I sit in my car for a while, writing down what I saw. A black SUV circles twice, waiting for me to leave.

❧

As landscapes diminish, every generation has to unlearn the previous generation's normal. When species like horseshoe crabs decline in Long Island Sound, their presence is no longer casual. What might once have been extricable, observational, parallel to human experience, is now deeply intertwined. There's no primeval other, no living fossil moving back and forth across the intertidal zone. Instead, we have a chain of relationships and reactions—horseshoe to Cancerine to lysate to bait—a mise en abyme where humans look back at a narrowing view of ourselves.

For years, I wanted my thinking to be like a drop of oil falling in water—touch the surface and a skin of interlinked circles prolifer-ates. As I grew up in marshlands, I imagined horseshoe crabs in the depths of Long Island Sound, swimming with ancient fishes, fil-tering sediment, pushing themselves at the advent of the full moon onto the shore of an ancient country, a borderless place that bore no resemblance to the suburbs of my childhood. In short, I imag-ined *limulus* romantic—and wild. But in these same moments, they were in biomedical laboratories, their telsons folded, a needle in each of their hearts like a plug in a socket. They were being har-vested with trawlers, cut up for bait, piled on top of one another in bins, overheated, sometimes breaking their shells or being stabbed in close quarters by the sharp points of other crabs. For my entire childhood, an extractive process was happening all up and down the coast where I lived, and I had known nothing about it. Let fall a drop of fact in memory and the truth will unsettle your mind.

By the end of the First World War, Fritz Haber was helping to de-velop mustard gas, which medical researchers later developed into chemotherapy treatments for cancer patients. Some of these are still used today. Each batch is tested with horseshoe crab lysate. And after the crabs are harvested, stacked, after the needle is inserted and blue blood spurts into the canisters, then—and only then—can all this stunned entanglement scuttle back into the deep.

5

Safer Skies for All Who Fly

Because we are optimistic, because we choose Providence, because we want to "build a life together." Because I commit to a job in nearby Boston that promises to support my writing. Because on Matt's first day at RISD no one remembers to introduce him to all his assembled colleagues and I can feel the pinch in my chest that means this is *not a good sign*, that means this place may spit us right back out. Because two-body problem, because the house we rent is falling apart at the gutters and full of mice, because they chew the wires and the kitchen begins to smoke while Matt is at work, dealing with a department that is imploding. Because the roof leaks and the water ruins most of his earliest paintings. Because he goes back on the market and gets an offer in Buffalo, because he wants to *get out of here*, because he signs a new contract the same month my job in Boston is starting. Because I can lose one city after another but I can't abandon the idea of a home for us, someday, together. For all these reasons, I am in the air again.

This time I fly to visit the kingdom of work, not love, though work is something I am capable of loving. For two days a week, I stay in Boston, and the rest of the time I am remote. This time there are no stories over the phone and I take pills to fall asleep. Every Monday, through the predawns of winter, Matt pulls us out of bed and drives me to the airport at 4 a.m., so I can fly to Boston in time for the first classes of the day. When I get there, the intern I hire tells me that I am a "work warrior," but I know I am slipping. In the morning I look in the mirror and my eyelids are puffed like those of a turtle or sea creature, and I dip my fingers in the cold faucet water and hold them up to my face.

I am in the air twice a week, but the dynamics of flight never completely lose their sense of the uncanny, no matter how much I think about physics, g-forces, the "stomach drops" of roller-coaster loops. The more I fly, the more I notice how the snow at takeoff is horizontal, revealing the speed of the plane. As my gaze plummets over the winter fields, the landscape flattens into a quilt of human purposes: towns, roads, tractor patterns, the odd swath of arborvitae between a subdivision and a highway. And between the floor of the cabin and the ground, the invisible pressure of the void, keeping the wings afloat.

One evening when I am in Buffalo, I realize that our new house sits directly beneath a crow flight path. We stand in a neighbor's yard, and for ten whole minutes we crick our necks to watch them passing, an uninterrupted stream of wings outlined against the oncoming night. We watch until our heads feel heavy with the pressure of looking up, but still, more crows appear over the tree line—flocks in the back roughly following the arc of the ones in front. At four hundred I stop counting to wonder if they'll roost somewhere in Buffalo tonight, if the neighborhoods to the east of the city will wake up under a blanket of raucous black wings.

After that, I see them each time I'm home, following the same route over the river. Under the cloudcap of winter, their feathered forms stand out like shapes cut into the vapor, a preview of the darkening sky behind. They become part of how I understand the days when the light fades early—crow flights: time to feed the dogs, time to listen for the soft sound of the car radio in the driveway. They induce a sense of homing. The opposite of an ill omen.

Yet I know that in their transits of the city, there's one place to the east of the river where they won't be welcome. At the Buffalo Niagara International Airport, such a large flock could seriously disrupt planes at takeoff and landing. In the environmental overview of this airfield, the writers warn of all the wildlife that might be present and that the airport would need to monitor: coyotes, white-tailed deer, foxes, "heavy concentrations" of pigeons, starlings, and either crows or blackbird species.

Biologist Richard Dolbeer reasons that the first bird to be hit by a plane was a redwing blackbird. In 1905, it met the top of the Wright brothers' aircraft during a flight over a cornfield in Ohio. Needless to say, the bird did not survive the encounter. As Wilbur Wright wrote in his diary, the carcass landed "on top of upper surface and after a time fell off when swinging a sharp curve." This incident marked a shift in the kind of spaces humans could occupy—as Dolbeer puts it, "Birds, which had been practicing powered flight for about 150 million years, suddenly had a new 'competitor' for airspace."

When a plane hits a bird or a flock, it's called a bird strike, and it happens every day. In 2021, the Federal Aviation Administration reported a total of 15,556 bird strikes with civilian aircraft. Most strikes from the last thirty years occurred during takeoff and landing, although the highest-reported collision was nearly at cruising altitude. Only a small fraction of these collisions result in any damage to the plane, and very few require it to land. But for the birds, the consequences are gruesome, especially if they collide with the engine turbines and are "ingested," which is the technical term. What's left is a mess of feathers, blood, and goo, which is called snarge (short for snot garbage).

These days, engines are *built* to withstand ingesting birds—they can churn through smaller species without harming the plane. But flocks and heavier birds are more likely to cause strike damage. There's even a testing device called a rooster booster or chicken gun that hurls chickens of various weights into parts of an aircraft to test their resilience to bird strikes. Thanks to this innovation, you could be on a plane that hits a bird and never know. In fact, if you fly a lot, you may well have been a passenger during a bird strike—without ever registering any disruption.

The more I flew, the more I began to wonder if, on one of those dark mornings, I might have been the human half of a human-wildlife conflict. For the curious, this information is readily available. The Federal Aviation Administration maintains an online database of airplane wildlife strikes, and anyone can search it. When I type in my local airport in Buffalo, each row in the database unveils a small story, a crossing of unlikely paths. Gulls hit by a 737, a red fox caught by a JetBlue flight. A kestrel and Southwest Airlines. Eventually I find my way back to the winter of 2018, to the black exhaustion of those winter dawns.

On December 3 of that year, I fly out of the Buffalo airport as usual, hoping to be in Boston in time for my 9 a.m. meeting. That day, there's a yellow-eyed ghost in the columns of the spreadsheet, which is the last place you'd want to see a migrant snowy owl, down from the Canadian Arctic. The database doesn't list which flight struck the owl, which meant the bird was likely identified from snarge or as a carcass on the airport grounds—white feathers against the white of a winter runway. There was nothing unusual about takeoff that day. But still, it could have been my flight.

The last time bird strikes entered the popular imagination was on January 15, 2009, when US Airways flight 1549 hit a flock of

Canada geese and ditched in the Hudson River. The pilot, Chesley Sullenberger, lost power to both engines after they ingested the birds. Surrounded by densely populated areas and unable to return to LaGuardia, he landed in the water. In the highly publicized photos of the accident, the passengers stand on the plane wings in the middle of the river, awaiting rescue by nearby boaters. Thanks to Sullenberger's decision-making, all 155 people on board the flight survived—the "miracle on the Hudson."

In the aftermath of this incident, the term "bird strike" seemed to invite a strange reversal of agency—as the faster, heavier, and bigger players in these conflicts, planes usually strike birds, not the other way around. If they can, birds initiate swerves and other predator-avoidance movements in response to aircraft—one study found they are often struck as they dive to get out of the way.

But as scholar Christopher Schaberg argues, through a kind of anthropomorphizing of the flock involved in the accident, the press began to give the birds an agency they didn't possess. Schaberg points specifically to a CNN article on the tenth anniversary of flight 1549 that says the birds "flew into" the engines, as if they'd wanted to be ingested. The article continues, calling the accident "a disturbing reminder to air travelers: We're not the only creatures in the sky." What this "confounding as-if epiphany" tells Schaberg is that such rhetoric can do "violence to basic ecological awareness, bundling an anthropocentric mindset into the viral buzz of news."

If a lack of ecological awareness is the symptom, its root causes are deeper and more slippery. Treating a disruption of the anthropocentric mind-set as a "disturbing reminder" tells me that perhaps there is a category of "open air" that parallels the myth of the open road. While radar can pick up other inhabitants of the sky, flocks of birds and swarms of insects are usually edited out as "noise" in the weather data. Yet there are many kinds of life in the air when you stop to think about it—the spores of fungi that help to seed clouds, the pollen, the bacteria. The airspace itself is shaped by what passes through it at a given moment—migrating cold fronts, winds from the desert, volcanic ash, jet trails, the seasonal movements of birds. If the skies as you approach the airport look empty, it's not an accident—airports often employ biologists and other wildlife management personnel to prevent birds and other animals from coming near airport runways. This line of work is called wildlife hazard mitigation, and it involves a host of strategies. Because passengers depend on flying safely, airport employees are busy keeping birds away.

How do you create a landscape of fear in the grammar of another species? It depends, first of all, on identifying which animals you're trying to scare. Sometimes it's as simple as letting the grass grow long, so that starlings will avoid a field that might camouflage a predator. Other times, the lawn needs to be treated along the runway edges so that earthworms don't crawl on the tarmac and lure robins to land. Shooting geese with paintball guns can be a nonlethal, stinging deterrent. If airport employees can't keep diamondback terrapins from entering the airport area, they will trap them and relocate them outside the fence. For deer that get through the chain-link, wildlife managers usually have permits to cull.

Airports also try to work with the surrounding areas to make them less attractive to animals. Removing trees, diverting sources of water, and carefully managing trash and other food sources can make a place unwelcoming to birds and wildlife. But one of the best methods is to have actual humans walking around—a predator in the form of an airport biologist.

After flight 1549 ditched in the Hudson, the Port Authority made a statement about their "zero tolerance policy" for geese on airport property. Beyond the runways themselves, more than 1,200 Canada geese were rounded up and gassed in the New York area. Wildlife managers also coated goose eggs in corn oil to prevent oxygen from getting through the shell—a way to keep the bird embryos from developing into hatchlings. (This method is considered more effective and humane than simply destroying the nests, since birds will continue to incubate the coated eggs, even though they cannot hatch, rather than laying a new clutch.) By the numbers, wildlife managers insist that all this isn't so bad—they kill only a tiny fraction of resident species.

But behind the curtain of this kind of public-facing language, further analysis of the goose feathers from the engines of flight 1549 revealed that they were from a flock of migratory birds outside their breeding range—a completely different population from the geese that were nesting in the area. Were the resident geese killed after the accident in part as a show of control? To help people feel more comfortable about flying?

As a child, I used to love taking the red-eye across the Atlantic the few times we visited my father's family in England. I would keep the shade open through the whole night, to see what the air had in store for us, like the particular tint of pink when clouds are lit from below, or the veil of the aurora as we slipped north to catch the jet stream. Once, after landing in London, I saw my first snowy owl on the dawn airfield at Heathrow—my father peering over my shoulder, his face transfixed as the bird turned toward us, as it opened and closed its eyes. He explained that snowy owls like airfields because their open landscapes resemble tundra, but he might not have realized the danger—at no point did he mention that birds could get hit. When I think now about why I sometimes distrust my memory, it's perhaps because these moments contain an almost painful innocence, something carried over from his own childhood in a time of greater abundance. With him, there was no conflict on the airfield, only a chance to see wonders from the window of the plane, to study the ice crystals forming between the double panes of the portal, to watch the wings of the white owl lift.

As the weeks of my commute pass, I become a person who pretends that she can be loaded like luggage. I try to fall asleep in cabs, on airplanes, immediately after takeoff. Because I need to be in two places, I constantly check my phone for the problems that might be arising, at home, at work, and in my personal email inbox, where I am cultivating future projects so I can switch back to freelancing and stop getting on planes each week. When I come home and Matt touches my shoulders, I think about cold snow and feathered muscles and aluminum. But I don't remember anything else about the day a plane hit the owl because I was just trying to get through it, which is, in truth, no way to live.

Nearly four years after that cold December morning, I am in the basement of the Smithsonian National Museum of Natural History in the middle of a Thursday, searching for snowy owl snarge.

I've come from Buffalo to D.C., to the imposing fronts of the National Mall, in hopes of finding some trace of those feathers. For lack of a better option, I fly. After I leave the airport, I walk to the museum through streets of commuters, past the J. Edgar Hoover FBI Building and the pediments of the National Archives. As I approach the Mall, it's still early—only a few tourists peer through the railings, and the carousel is empty. To kill a little time, I wander through a pollinator garden that surrounds the Museum of Natural History, with fresh placards about the native species of D.C.—the coneflowers that feed finches, the wax myrtle berries that help overwintering flocks. You wouldn't guess from the outside that the mail for this building is full of the pulverized remnants of birds.

Despite its invisibility to everyday travelers, there is a whole facility here designed to classify and catalog birds that are hit by airplanes, including those that were ingested by the engines of flight 1549.

Once snarge is wiped off a plane or collected from the ground, pilots and airport personnel can address it to a facility in the museum called the Feather Identification Lab. This team of forensic ornithologists uses visual identification, DNA analysis, and microscopic properties of feathers to figure out what kind of creature got hit. The data they gather helps inform what kinds of bird strikes occur in different parts of the country, and which deterrents airports should use to keep wildlife away from their properties. The lab counts on airport employees and pilots to send in the bird fragments they find—meaning that the scientists performing the research on bird strikes rely on those who kill the birds to provide the material evidence for their investigations. The data the Feather Lab gathers is included in the Federal Aviation Administration wildlife-strike database and shared with wildlife managers at airports.

In the case of that snowy owl strike, only the date, the airport, and the bird species were included in the public database—not the airline, the time of day, or any other information. To find out more, I've come to see (the very appropriately named) Carla Dove, a forensic ornithologist and program manager of the Feather Identification Lab. She's warm and rigorous—plowing through the morning's email in Birkenstocks and bright green toenail polish. After I navigate museum security, she shows me into her office on a floor below the public halls of dinosaur bones and dioramas where schoolchildren and curious adults can see taxidermized tigers, an insect zoo, and a wing of fossils called Deep Time.

Against her office wall, a bookcase holds bird guides from all over the world. One poster reads: *Did it ever happen? Report all strikes!* Another: *Safer skies for all who fly.* Before I even arrived, she told me that in the wake of flight 1549, people started to look at the wildlife-strike database when they were booking plane tickets, choosing airports that had fewer bird strikes. But that's not really the right way to think about it—as a passenger, you actually want to fly somewhere that is actively reporting strikes and using that information to try to mitigate bird-airplane collisions. A robust list of bird strikes in the database means that airport employees are paying attention to which birds are in the area, so they can create informed plans for how to protect both humans and birds. "If you see no bird strikes, you don't want to fly there," Dove puts it. "Because I guarantee you, they're happening."

For her, the puzzle of unraveling these encounters is what keeps her coming back to this work. When I say I might have been on a plane that struck a bird, her face becomes focused—a sleuth on the trail of a case. Did the owl snarge pass through her hands? A few clicks later, she tells me yes, it did, and they identified it with DNA analysis. What's more, the collision damaged the plane—which means they might still have the original sample the pilot sent. To find out, Dove says, with a slight gleam in her eye, we'll have to visit the basement. "Uh-oh," her research assistant says. Another colleague warns us that the lights in their section of the storage area have gone out. My headlamp is still in my bag from the horseshoe crab survey, and I offer to wear it, like a spelunker in the middle of a city of suits. Then we set out, down the stairs into the cavernous subfloors that used to be the museum's parking garage.

I'm trying, with this visit, to get back to the animal beginnings of things. Back to the pocket of air beneath his wings as he banks for a landing, to the way each feather cuts an infinite slice of sky. To the owl on the airfield, hunting with acute yellow eyes for rodents under the windswept snow. To the commuter body, buckling in for a flight. To what happens after the first moment of collision—the people in gloves, holding the spent fragments of a bird.

When animal remains are discovered at the airport, the process depends on the initial details. Sometimes airport biologists can identify the species involved in a strike as it happens, and they report it to the Federal Aviation Administration database then and there. If there's a carcass that the airport employees can't identify, the Feather Lab requests a selection of whole feathers from different parts of the bird, especially feathers that reveal a distinctive color or pattern. When there's less to go on—a few feathers, say, or some blood—the lab requests the downy part of the feather, or a bit of tissue that's wiped with alcohol and dried, which makes a good sample for DNA analysis. ("If you see a dried scab, give it to me," Dove says, and laughs.)

After snarge is collected with a plastic bag, it's shipped in an ordinary envelope, through the postal service, or through a faster carrier if the identification is urgent. These packages—labeled "safety investigation material"—travel from airports all over the US to the storied columns of this museum row. The day I was there, the lab received 104 submissions of bird strike remains, though at the very peak of migration season, the number can be even higher.

Every case is different. It's easiest if an envelope contains intact feathers—then Dove and her team can take that feather into the Smithsonian's vast collection, where six hundred thousand specimens of birds are available for comparison, in drawers just outside the door of their lab. Many of these specimens were collected before airplanes even existed, before birds had "competition" for airspace. After looking through samples of whole hawks or killdeer or gulls, preserved as flat "skins" in the museum's cabinets, Dove can match the feathers in her hand to the patterns of a species, holding the struck bird's feather up to a whole tail to check her hunch.

If there's only tissue or blood splatter or a bit of feather in the envelope, the team relies on properties of the sample that aren't visible to the naked eye, like DNA. But the lab's original method, and one they still use, involves a kind of transfiguration—from a scrap caught in the fuselage to something else entirely.

The process begins with the downy barbs of a feather: the fluffy tendrils close to the base of the quills. This down is not usually from flight feathers but from those that line the body of a bird and help keep it warm. First, the staff washes these pieces, removing blood, "bird ick," and engine oil. Then they place a barb on a slide and look at it under a microscope. Suspended under the lens, the barbs branch into even tinier filaments, called barbules. They tangle like grasses when they're backlit at evening, licked in one direction by the rising wind.

As these filaments of feather extend, they're punctuated by nodes—microscopic bumps that reveal clues about what kind of bird they once belonged to. On a living bird, these nodes help to knit the down of their plumage together. With snarge, these microscopic characteristics help to narrow identification to a particular category. Waterfowl have triangular nodes. The nodes of crow feathers are dark, with their signature black pigment. Pigeons and doves have barbules dotted with crocus shapes, flared flowers around a stem. Owls have nodes like bells whose tongues are wispy strands of hair. I was unprepared for how beautiful they are.

I don't know very many people who can identify a bird based just on location and the microscopic characteristics of its feathers. But sometimes things get even more complicated. Early in our conversation, Dove tells me about one of the strangest cases she's encountered. One January, when the lab had just started using DNA analysis, they received material from a bird strike. When the results of the sample came back, they identified a white-tailed deer. On the surface, that wasn't unheard-of, since planes can hit deer while taxiing. But when Dove looked at the report, she saw that the strike had occurred 1,500 feet above the ground. Despite the proximity to Christmas, no one in the lab wanted to believe hoofed creatures were circling in the skies. So they analyzed the DNA sample three more times, and three more times it came back the same.

At that point, Dove decided to resort to the classic methods. As she puts it, "mind over molecule." They got in touch with the airport that had sent in the strike to ask if perhaps they'd made a mistake in the report, if the strike had actually happened when the plane was still on the runway. But no, the pilot was adamant—he'd been in the air, and the strike had made a twenty-thousand-dollar hole in the wing.

There was nothing left to do but make a slide and see what was visible under the microscope. Among the deer hairs, Dove tells me, was the barb of a feather. By looking at the barbules, they were eventually able to identify the bird as a black vulture. That's when the pieces started falling into place. The bird—a scavenger—must have been feeding on a deer carcass before it flew into the air and was hit by the plane. The vulture's crop was full of deer remains.

"We would get all these great identifications," Dove says of the DNA analysis, "so when this came back, of course, we believed it. But we just weren't thinking about the whole case and all of the circumstances." Since then, they've had a couple of cases like that, where DNA from snakes and other prey appeared at higher altitudes. Now the lab knows it's probably because these ground-dwelling animals were in the talons (or the stomach) of a bird. But it takes long experience to reach these answers.

~

Dove's colleagues were right—this is an extremely haunted basement. We walk through a maze of right angles, past a model triceratops jaw, plaster lumps of stabilized fossils, disintegrating dried plants, bits of building material. "Are those branches or tusks?" Dove asks, as we pass a dusty cart from the paleontology department. It's clear that few people have been down here recently—when we reach the storage area and push open the door, its laminated label cracks and falls to the ground. The lights are indeed out, and I hold my headlamp high so Dove can thumb through the files.

Within the cabinet itself, meticulous order reigns. Or maybe it's the kind of order that appears perfect because it's been reclaimed from chaos. *Lots of damage!!!* notes one strike report, in someone's alarmed handwriting. *Plane is totaled.*

As Dove pages through the records, I notice that each report is stapled to a little plastic baggie of remains—feathers, blood on alcohol wipes—a filing cabinet full of collisions. "Let's see if we can find your owl," she says, and that *your* makes my hand shake as it holds the light—I don't know what it means, through curiosity or guilt, to have assumed ownership of these fragments.

But there is one person who might know. In Boston, at Logan airport, a self-taught naturalist and community scientist named Norman Smith has kept watch for decades with his children. As the weather gets colder and the snowy owls begin to arrive, he shows up at the airport each time he gets a call, to trap and relocate them away from the runways. "It is hard to imagine," he writes, "that a place like Logan Airport in East Boston, Massachusetts, with all its activity, megadecibel sounds, and constant jet fumes, provides one of the best locations in the state to encounter these magnificent raptors." In an article he wrote about his work, he includes a photo of his daughter and son, both holding snowy owls, poised to toss them back upward into the air.

On camera, his daughter, Danielle, looks about my age—a nineties kid in a parka, grinning and looking away from the slitted eyes of the raptor as her fingers wrap the underside of her wing. And

I realize that we've both been owling on the airfields with our bird-watcher fathers, but while I was a passenger, she was on the ground, our perspectives partitioned by the plexiglass windows of the plane.

In a good year, Norman and his kids have had to transport as many as forty owls to release them on the beaches of Duxbury or Salisbury. Before letting them go, he samples their blood to see what kind of toxins they have absorbed on their travels—rodenticide from eating airport rats, sometimes heavy metals, too. Because of how far the owls range, it's difficult to assess their population size, but the bird conservation network Partners in Flight estimates that since 1976, they've lost approximately two-thirds of their numbers. When the lemming population booms, the owls thrive through the long arctic summers, hunting in the perpetual daylight of the midnight sun. Their feathers keep them warm in the high arctic, providing pounds of insulation that cover the skin, even between their talons, making them the heaviest North American owls, a danger to airplanes. Each time Norman traps and removes one of these birds from Logan, he transforms the bird from a conflict back into an animal, preventing the kind of collision that happened on that dark runway in Buffalo.

For weeks, I watch videos on YouTube of Norman releasing the snowys—how they lift from his hands into the wind coming off the water, how the sand ripples beneath his feet like the flapping striations on their wings.

As it turns out, it wasn't my flight that hit the snowy owl that morning in 2018. According to the crash report, the bird bounced off the wing of a plane bound for LaGuardia, leaving a dent two feet wide. But the captain and the first officer agreed that the strike occurred on the dark, windy takeoff from Buffalo, before they landed in New York City at dawn. Neither one noticed the impact. After they landed, the pilot found evidence that the bird had been ingested into the #2 engine—he took a sample to send to the Feather Lab from the first-stage turbine blades.

I was there on the airfield, though, on a plane in the predawn hours, perhaps even queuing for takeoff when the strike took place. I would have liked to walk around, to see if the owl left a mark in the white with his talons, if his wings had touched down in powder before the track was erased. If I had looked hard enough, I might have seen him dive for a snowdrift with his wide, quiet reach.

No trace of the owl remains in the files either—the strike wasn't damaging enough for Dove and her colleagues to keep the snarge long-term. The original samples were sent, on what they call the "dead wagon," to the incinerator, where all the pulverized birds they've finished with are unraveled back into ash and sky.

Upstairs, I meet Dr. Faridah Dahlan, who handles DNA analysis for the lab. She pulls up "my" owl's sequence from her records and I see the markers of its particular proteins undulate across her screen—a long series of CATGATTGGAAACT. It's a beautiful, complete sequence, she says, and the closest I'll get to this particular creature today.

More than anything, the Feather Identification Lab is a sign of what it really takes to wedge an airport into a living ecosystem—and how hard it is to create a landscape that functions for human purposes alone. Dove comes in on weekends and holidays, and her lab was staffed through the pandemic. It's patient, often thankless work. One of the reasons they have to keep doing these identifications is that as species move and adapt to climate change, they show up outside their usual range. "In my thirty years of working here," Dove says, "we never used to get black vultures in the northern states. And now we do." When the makeup of species changes, wildlife management has to keep up—it's an endless push and pull that can stop only if flying does.

During the first year of the pandemic, bird strikes from civilian aviation did drop by about 30 percent, but they quickly returned to their previous highs. Despite this brief "anthropause," it seems the trend is more likely to move in the opposite direction—toward more planes, more drones, more light pollution—in short, more human presence in airspace.

If flight is on the rise, why don't people talk about the ecological work it requires? Why do our mental images of airports include baggage handlers and copilots, catering and refueling, control towers and workers in bright vests with flares to direct pushback from the gate—and not the meticulous process of identifying birds from snarge, or the biologists who keep wildlife away? Though loneliness is a response to isolation from other species, isolation can also be maintained as a defense mechanism. I suspect the human-wildlife conflicts of air travel are rarely acknowledged, because their invisibility is convenient. In 2013, an outcry erupted over the shooting of snowy owls at New York City airports. An illustration appeared in the *New York Daily News* showing an owl with red crosshairs over his face. After a petition gathered three thousand signatures, the Port Authority started a program to trap and relocate the birds instead. Strategies that help owls share the airspace may require more effort. But shying away from these aspects of daily airport operation creates a blind spot, a hidden obstacle with the potential to shock.

As the morning advances, Dove lets me shadow her as she begins to solve the day's cases. The smell, as she opens the baggies of snarge, is rank, a little rotten. The kind of odor my cat would love. Some of the feathers have been churned, their quills broken.

Others are intact. Dove opens a bag and sniffs—it's salty, probably osprey. We're standing at a table in a pool of fluorescent light, surrounded by floor-to-ceiling specimen drawers. She pulls one open to reveal scarlet tanagers at every stage of their plumage.

Next, Dove pulls out a darker feather with a dab of white in the middle. She asks me what I think it is, and I tell her that if I had to guess, I'd say it belonged to a mockingbird. But she shakes her head. "The feathers are so soft," she says. We take turns touching the tip of the feather where it still bears the white crescent of a recent molt. The texture feels elegant, like heavy, expensive paper. She tells me that the softness itself is a clue—longer barbules mean the feather belonged to a night bird, one that hunts in the dark. We walk down the aisles, to the section of nightjars who catch insects on quiet wings, especially when the moon is high. I tell her about the last time I stayed in the woods, how I heard the whip-poor-will calling through the skylight as I slept. She says she used to listen for that call because when she was a child, it was a sign of warmer weather—if the whip-poor-will sang, her mother would let her play barefoot.

Just next to the whip-poor-wills are the common nighthawks. Dove unfolds a wing and finds the perfect match for her snarge.

"Here," she says to me, pulling a strike from Texas out of the pile. "You can get this one." In the ziplock bag, there's a wing, no longer than my thumb, with tiny scales of green sequin at the shoulder. It can only be a hummingbird.

I ask Dove and her colleagues if they ever get sad about a hummingbird strike, and she admits they do. After all, she is working at an uneasy intersection between the behavior of humans and birds. Which is not to say they are always weighted equally.

"Everybody sort of focuses on this as a human safety issue . . . ," Dove tells me. "But I always tell people, if we can keep the birds away from the airports, we are saving birds." The conservation potential of her work is particularly significant in choosing sites for new runways. Many existing airfields are located along flyways that millions of birds pass through during fall and spring migrations. Others, like John F. Kennedy International Airport, are built near protected areas, basically guaranteeing a strong presence of wildlife. Despite the expertise of biologists on the ground, Dove tells me they're often excluded from the decisions about where to propose or expand an airport.

I ask her what she'd advise a planner looking to site new infrastructure. "Don't build the airport near a river, don't build the airport near a garbage dump, and don't build the airport near a wildlife refuge," she says. "But they still do it."

Sometimes, as in the case of the hummingbird, there might not be much wildlife managers can do to deter the species from the airfield. But the Feather Identification Lab still wants a record of those strikes. In a country where accidental wildlife loss often goes unnoticed or unreported, the Feather Lab is a rare exception. The data that Dove and her colleagues provide offers a window into the fraught relationship between migrating birds and airfields— information that can be used to justify both culling and conservation. Without the Feather Lab's efforts, people wouldn't know what they were hitting, and there would be many more small birds whose journeys meet with a plane's wing and suddenly go silent. This lab is one place where absences can be counted, where the fallout from human-wildlife conflicts is investigated and cataloged. The goal, as Dove puts it, is separation: "to keep birds and people apart, so birds can live, too."

⌁

I know what it's like to feel separate, to be floating through the dark sky wrapped in a ship of aluminum, to sense the pressure changes, the stale cabin air coming in and out of your body. To be unreachable for hours, while everything is moving beneath you, while your partner goes about his morning, drinks coffee in the sun puddle coming through the window, while he takes the dog for a walk and talks with a neighbor, while he washes his breakfast dishes. It's not just that you aren't home; it's that you're nowhere nearby, not even close, and that if love makes a tie between humans, each week you are stretching it, and even if it is flexible and strong, there isn't enough time, when you are together, for your tie to shrink back into the size of closeness, to absorb all that distance between you.

When I am in Buffalo, I begin to learn how to meditate, to hold as much of the atmosphere of our house in my body as I can, to make the air between us, the air of our shared space, just as much a part of me. Even so, Matt says I am not present enough. I am yoked to the in-between time of air travel, and the few clothes I scatter across our bedroom as I pack each week are less the traces of a human partner and more the graspings of an anxious ghost. To accommodate this commute, I am making my own life smaller, even as my ecological footprint grows. I push away the animal of my body and all other animals, too, traveling so light that even when I am on the ground, I am not solid—I can inhale the air and hold it but I don't have the right ballast, I am not carrying enough of my home.

One day, I'm too tired to talk, and I snap at him on the way to the airport. Then he goes quiet, and in that silence I feel the stiff breeze of a terrible freedom, as if one *shut up* could cut me loose.

❧

Part of the difficulty with bird-aircraft collisions is that for a long time, humans didn't recognize the airspace itself as a habitat. There is no way for creatures to mark it as their territory. And the life of organisms that drift on the wind is often invisible. The conditions of their endurance evolve through unseen and unstable forces— the temperature and the wind and the weather. But the consensus about airspace is changing. Birds perceive much more in the sky than we can—relying on polarized light, the Earth's magnetic field, and subtle shifts in the density of air. Recent research has determined that swifts can spend entire months at a time on the wing—getting everything they need from the aerosphere, even a place to sleep. Parts of this habitat are ephemeral but no less real because they are imperceptible to humans. Raptors, for example, can rise on thermals, hovering in the afternoon on warm currents of air that vanish when night falls. Flying creatures often aren't territorial about their pieces of sky, because there's no reason to be— when the airspace offers a swarm of insects or a favorable tailwind, these resources feel practically unlimited.

To understand the aerosphere better, I spoke to Benjamin Van Doren at the Cornell Lab of Ornithology. He'd recently published a paper in the *Proceedings of the National Academy of Sciences* about the migrating birds who are attracted, each fall, to the Tribute in Light at Ground Zero. Using radar from weather stations, he and his co-author examined how the illumination of these floodlights was pulling in thousands of migrating birds each year—that the draw of this human memorial was creating a serious conflict, disorienting flying creatures in a zone of light-polluted air.

In the course of our conversations, both Dove and Van Doren brought up radar, which could help planes avoid birds before they're close enough to collide. At the Cornell Lab of Ornithology, Van Doren has been involved in a project called BirdCast, which uses radar to predict when the heaviest concentrations of migrating birds will be airborne. Many birds migrate at night, and weather data disregards the "noise" of these flights. But Van Doren and his colleagues have flipped it—they remove weather patterns from radar to look at the trajectories of birds.

Just like meteorologists, Van Doren and his colleagues "ground-truth" their data—with eBird, a community science bird-watching project. He and his colleagues have argued for simple changes to human behavior during the days when millions of birds travel through these corridors of sky. Just a few nights of turning off lights in skyscrapers can make a major difference. So could a few evenings of tweaked flight schedules. If we can see flocks of crows moving over an airport in near real time, wouldn't it make sense to wait till they've passed, like a transient thunderstorm?

When I ask him about the potential impacts of BirdCast, Van Doren points to the ways radar can show where birds are stopping, to prioritize the habitats that sustain them along their journeys. But then he tells me about another aspect of aeroecology, which I haven't stopped thinking about since. Part of what his research recognizes is that habitat loss isn't just a phenomenon that takes place on the ground. "As more vehicles and structures and light . . . reach into the atmosphere," Van Doren says, "that airspace is less often considered as a habitat itself. But it's an important one for lots of animals." What's developing through aeroecology is an understanding that humans have been slow to perceive the aerial world as a place of sustenance, because the way of life it offers is so opaque to us and so different from our own. Aeroecologists and sky conservationists study how airborne creatures perceive disruptions to their world—of celestial patterns, of magnetic fields, of flight—rather than focusing solely on the places where they return to land.

As we're wrapping up, Van Doren shows me the map of radar stations, green dots all across the US. On a peak migration night in May, the movements of flocks pulse through the air around the arrays like so many night-blooming flowers. Or, as Van Doren puts it, "like a heartbeat of migratory birds."

After I leave the Feather Lab, I take a cab back to the airport, crossing the bridge over the Potomac River. The sun has come out, and the runways shimmer in the early September heat. I walk around the terminal, staring out through the plate glass windows. Though I look for birds, I'm relieved not to see a single one. I watch for a while as the planes heave themselves out of their shadows. Then, in the airport bathroom, I wash the last touch of the nighthawk's feather off my hand.

6

Vertical Time

A man stands at the edge of the highway, pulled over between LA and Phoenix to watch flocks of birds lift out of the hills. As he swings his gaze across lanes of traffic, his binoculars catch blips of white in a dusty landscape: cigarette butts at the edge of the road. Though he's trying to immerse himself among convenience stores and gas pumps, his accent gives him away. He's been here nine years, and he's still a "resident alien"—a British man road-tripping all the way from California to Connecticut, on the highways of 1984. From each leg of his trip, he writes a postcard to two married friends in London, who can only answer to his final destination: Rural Route Box 129, West Cornwall, CT. If he wants their replies, he'll have to drive some 3,400 miles.

Before he leaves, he sends a first message in blue ink on blue airmail paper. He encloses a photograph, prefiguring the postcard theme. It's not a great shot—LA from above, looking down toward La Brea, where tar pits were once quarried to build city roads. Perhaps it's impossible to capture the image of leavetaking unless the photo is flawed. The sky is white, overexposed, the towers hazy. The kind of photo a tourist would take, without reference to the nearby house where he's spent the last six years, the lemons planted, the ivied slope of the backyard. He's separating from his wife, giving her space, setting out after a night of conversations that hurt. On the eve of his departure, it's by no means a given that this man will become my father. Though he'll visit a few people when he stops to rest, he'll mostly have the accelerator to lean on, making the drive alone.

~

Before there was a road, there was its soft shoulder—the original cut that holds the asphalt's span. These earthworks open the landscape and help highways last through thousands of travelers and rainstorms. Shoulders collect the evidence of what's passed through, or the traces of what's discarded in the course of passage. Particulates, blown-out tires, dark tracks where a car hit the brakes and swerved. In most places, you can't touch the shoulder without the juddering exclamation of the rumble strip, enough to shake most drivers from their drift.

When passages collide, the shoulder collects the aftermath. The sudden movement of a deer who decides, at the wrong moment, to ford the river of wheels. The shattered reflectors. The black wings of crows or the vultures whose feathers sometimes crook like fingers, lifting from roadkill at the edge of the highway. The rank smell of skunk. But the strangest thing I've seen on the shoulder wasn't an animal at all but a haze of white fluff clinging to freshly resurfaced macadam, as if the road had been feathered, perhaps by a predator, a hawk with something pale in his talons. But when I looked closer, I saw that the fluff was attached to flat, round seeds— the tiny parachutes of milkweed, blown in the wake of a car.

Other creatures make paths through landscape that are more defined and repeatable than the intersection between a road and the prevailing wind. I'm thinking of tunnels made by wild pigs in undergrowth, or of deer trails crossing a hiking path. But it's dangerous to borrow such a road. Once, out for a run, I realized too late that I'd been lost for an hour in the transportation logic of another species, weaving through thin winter bracken. Eventually, the deer trail I'd been following reached 146, a route I knew, though I didn't immediately recognize it, having never before stood at this intersection where a wild thoroughfare crossed the human. I found myself panting at the edge, where a deer would stand, surveying the cars for an opening.

For years, from apartment to apartment, I've been carrying the postcards my father sent from the road. Last winter, on a bright day after a storm, I slid them out onto my desk. Then I picked up the first card and stared at it, the quiet air caught in my throat—

It was February 3 at my desk in Buffalo. And February 3 in his first message. And I realized I'd been handed a rare invitation to retrace the days of his drive nearly forty years later—that even from afar, even just mapping the lines of his journey, I could feel an impossible overlap as I wrote, our Februarys touching, a chance to reach across the intervening decades. If I wanted, I could trespass a little on the paths he traveled before I knew him, when the life my parents made had become unsettled, when it wasn't clear if he and my mother would make a family or if this country would always be his home.

During that dystopian year of 1984, John Berger published a book of vignettes called *And Our Faces, My Heart, Brief as Photos*, a book whose title has always reminded me of postcards. Here, he attempts a human definition of home as the crux between horizontal and vertical time. For him, "the horizontal line represented the traffic of the world, all the possible roads leading across the earth to other places," and the vertical line represented the ancestral time of the graveyard and the layers of accumulated generations going deep into the Earth. With an awareness of this intersection, Berger writes, people could be at home even while in motion. But to lose access to the vertical was to feel the world fragment and become unmoored, lonely, absurd. "My view of time," he writes, ". . . is being remorselessly cross-examined by death."

There is still so much I don't know about my father's February, the thoughts that passed through his mind over long highway miles, through the shortest, the hungriest, month. His first post-card shows a triad of glossy saguaros retreating into the distance. "L.A. to Phoenix," he writes. "400 miles of desert. Suddenly, in the middle of nowhere, a huge gathering of caravans and camp-ers, like a flock of migrant birds." Did he see, in this simile, the cyclical movements of seasons, the glimmer of a future return? It's a stretch, I know, to read into the past like that. He was always the one to swim to the island, wander a little farther, hike out alone—a watcher, someone who turned himself outward. A man who had no fear of travel except in the passport control lines at airports, when I would feel his hand sweat as it held mine. What, in 1984, would home have meant to him?

A pronghorn's home is the route it walks, a traveling residence interrupted by the infrastructure of human habitats. Thanks to GPS collars, you can watch as these animals unravel the paths where they live, navigating old routes north and south that cross some of the nation's busiest highways. A feature by Ben Guarino in the *Washington Post* details the journey of pronghorn 700031A as she grazed her way south across Wyoming, moving down to her winter habitat. She begins as a small purple dot on the map, suc-cessfully crossing several roads on her way south, before stopping, trapped by Route 80. Against the vast landscape of sagebrush, the long fences of barbed wire might look minimal to drivers. But pronghorn don't like to jump fences and often get fatally tangled

even before they reach the traffic. Many choose not to risk crossing at all. Just north of the highway, the map becomes hazy with
purple dots—the overlapping paths of all the collared pronghorn
stuck above this barrier.

Some still try to brave these intersections, to follow the same routes
their ancestors did. Pronghorn are ruminants—the last living members of the Antilocapridae family—and the wildlife corridors they
travel are thousands of years old, existing far longer than the highways. In their travels, these ungulates catch what biologists call the
"green wave," riding the swell of vegetation to their summer pas-
tures and slowing when grazing is plentiful. They don't move just
to get somewhere—instead, the paths themselves are their means
of survival.

I'm picking up my mother from a friend's house, driving her home
through marshland. This winter—4 p.m., dark already—she no
longer wants to drive at night. It's cataracts, she tells me, they
exacerbate the glare of oncoming cars. There is no public transit
where she lives, and when I'm not around, I worry that this new
development is isolating her. As we cross from ghost forest into living woods, I spot something—four legs, fur—darting across the
road up ahead. I slow down, and there, in a neighbor's driveway,
the eyeshine of a coyote flashes back. Did you see that? I ask my
mother, and she shakes her head. She needs eye surgery, she says;
the doctor thinks she's ready for it, and I wonder again about these
roadside places, about how much more is happening here than we
perceive.

"You road I enter upon and look around, I believe you are not all
that is here," writes Walt Whitman. "I believe that much unseen is
also here." Collisions between humans and other animals are often
overlooked—especially at highway speeds. But in the hit-and-run

world of wildlife loss, other species usually wind up dead, while sometimes people don't even register the impact. Human roads, and especially highways, insist on this kind of exceptional right to pass through the landscape unimpeded. It's a deer problem, not a highway problem. In this sense, a road shoulder isn't just a receptacle or a safety feature. It's a wedge that pushes through a crowd, shoving everyone else out of the way.

To drive west to east is to feel the horizon narrow, to anticipate the cluttered skyscape of the Northeast Corridor, the slow cocooning of New England's tree-lined roads. Driving eastward moves against the grain of genocidal American mythmaking, retracing, backward, the violence of Manifest Destiny. Phoenix, Santa Fe, Forth Smith—it's clear from his postcards that my father's journey followed Route 66 through the Southwest, the so-called "Mother Road" that had recently become I-40.

Did my father know what he was driving? Stopping in Santa Fe, he notes the "uncomfortable" tourist attractions—cowboy stereotypes of the Old West. Apart from that one moment, there aren't many clues to his mind's interior. By February 9, I can feel him picking up speed—he was in Shamrock, Texas, where everything he saw skewed toward temporary. "The Texas panhandle is flat, treeless," he writes on the back of a windmill pumping water for cattle. "Small, featureless, scraggly towns, all motel and gas station signs, as if they existed only for those passing through." I can imagine my father's good friends in London receiving this missive with some concern, wondering if these postcards were working as a hedge against the sure loneliness of the road. He tells them what he listens to on the radio, what he watches on the small motel TV. As he writes, late at night or early in the morning, in the moments when he's not wrapped by the frame of the car, his friends keep him company in shabby suites with empty pools out the window, concrete basins drained and covered for winter. Sometimes it's enough to send a message to keep yourself from feeling alone. By the time his friends read a postcard, he's already somewhere else. Mostly, my father turns his dispatches away from himself—by profession he's a sociologist who first came to America as a researcher, someone who specializes in loss and uncertainty. These outposts are the kinds of places he liked to write about, interviewing the very real people whose livelihoods get made or unmade by new infrastructure, the decisions of faraway planners, the workings of eminent domain.

Later, at my mother's house, I find the slides from his trip and lift each one up to the skylight, almost like I'm peering through a shutter. A vista of snow, desert, and wire. A lake of mud. Willows scrawled over a picnic table. It's not much, but I'm grateful for the evidence of his crossing, for the idiosyncrasy of what stood out to him when he flipped through these precarious highway verges like pages in a half-read book. The postcards from 1984 reach out across the intervening years with their airmail stamps—*first, fast and reliable*—a sign the line between us isn't dead.

It's easy to forget that roads have vertical time, too—that the frantic horizontal movements they enable hide both historical and archaeological records. In truth, many highways and roads in the US still follow trails that were built by Indigenous peoples. The highway my father drove is no exception. Though the origins of I-40 are often attributed to Edward Beale, who surveyed the route in the late 1850s with a team of camels imported from Tunisia, that story erases the older paths crossing the Southwest and linking traditional homelands. In Texas and Oklahoma, for example, scholar and artist Jimmy W. Arterberry has helped document how Comanche tied leather thongs around trees to sculpt them into living wayfinding markers, training their branches to mark a river crossing, water source, hunting area, or burial ground. Though the trunks are old now and some have been toppled by the weather, Comanche elders in Texas still held a recent ceremony to recognize one particular tree, whose branches make the sharp ninety-degree angle that signals the deep roots of this path.

Then there is the makeup of the asphalt itself, a reminder that both the surface under the wheels and the gas in the tank were baked in the geological strata. Asphalt is a naturally occurring substance, a form of crude oil, the same ooze that occasionally seeped to the surface at La Brea and trapped predators like *Smilodon*, saber-toothed cats. Crude oil deposits are largely congealed from humbler life forms—diatoms, buried plankton mixed with sediments, remnants of ancient aquatic environments. Asphalt is a substrate of decayed ancient oceans, marshes, inland lakes. Under pressure and heat, over hundreds of millions of years, the remains of these tiny organic creatures become crude oil and natural gas—a massive reservoir that humans remove from its resting place and bring to the surface. Roads are fashioned from the depths of vertical time— and they represent its extraction and dispersal, the domestication of what's left of a previous ecosystem, a tamed slurry girdled by the double yellow line.

What survives from the depths, what surfaces? To drive on the highway is to inhabit the discontinuity between distracted daily experience and ancient agglomeration of decay—the diatoms that made up the layers of asphalt, what's left of a prehistoric ocean unearthed and cooked in a factory.

I felt that as I drove from Buffalo to Connecticut in the middle of our February, mirroring my father's route. I was headed there to help my mother with her cataract surgeries—first one eye and then, two weeks later, the other. In between, I'd stay nearby, in the same small wooden building my father had also chosen as his destination, driving through fallow fields toward the New England hills, toward the quiet cold of a one-room schoolhouse. He and my mother had fixed it up early in their marriage, when he'd longed for somewhere on the East Coast—a foothold halfway between LA and London, equipped with a loft for sleeping and the woodstove of a winter cabin. I was thinking about the trip's logistics when, just outside Rochester, the snow began—squalling the windshield at odd intervals from fast-passing clouds. A crow caught a down-draft and perched on the guardrail like a comma, a breath of black ruffling in the swirl. Before long, I passed a tangled car wreck that had caught fire on the shoulder, and I saw where the heat had melted the asphalt underneath, pooling the darkness into more than shadow. As I slipped past, I felt the sight of the wreck send tension up my spine, binding the stones of its vertebrae, as if to guard against the danger of the road.

People are sometimes closer to the terrain of the world than they would like to believe. Robert Macfarlane points out in his book *Underland* that human bodies have their own internal landscapes. "We are part mineral beings too—our teeth are reefs, our bones are stones—and there is a geology of the body as well as of the land." It's easy to associate oil and stone with the primordial, but less easy to think, in our own intimacy with roads, about the long time scales of the Earth—a verticality that travel can't outrun.

After February 13, there's a break in my father's communication— four days with no postcards. He had just left New York City, mail-ing an image of the Statue of Liberty. He was crossing the New York state line, turning away from the Hudson River toward Cornwall, a journey of only a hundred miles. But with a multitude of rural routes, I can't tell which road he chose—like so many turns in another's lifetime, this one can't be retraced. I do know he must have walked up hill to the schoolhouse—a place that smells of wet fieldstone and bayberry wax, with grassy wheel ruts that lead to the door. Did he sense, in the dun-colored meadow, the calls of jays, the tracks of porcupines and deer and foxes, all the possible trails that might intersect his footsteps before they disappeared into the woods? Or did his impression drift toward silence—hearing, in a quiet place, all the internal voices drowned by the tasks of the road?

If he arrived at night, when the trees are loud with eyes, did he feel a sense of isolation, the darkness of the night pressing on the roof? I never saw fear in him, only a drive to get out of the house, to find what the morning had translated: fresh snow and the puzzle of tracks, a bobcat who crossed the meadow while he was sleeping, placing her hind paw in the impression of the fore. And once you've seen a bobcat, it's impossible not to imagine the world as a map of tracks crossing—her silent trail through the woods, the underwing of the owl muffling its flight, and, for that matter, all the creatures making their way: what might have just missed you, or what might, in the course of an unknown trajectory, be headed toward your own.

In the late fall and early spring, I like to watch the live feed of the trail camera at Trapper's Point, a wildlife crossing over Wyoming's highway 191. Even if I don't catch a glimpse of anything moving on the slope, the hoofprints in the earth of the overpass are a sign of reconnected animal paths. These kinds of crossings are designed specifically to attract wildlife, either as overpasses (in the case of pronghorn) or as tunnels under the highway, to give animals a safe route across these roads. But well-placed crossings don't just allow animal populations to move between divided parts of their habitat. They also help humans imagine and value the ways other species have found a home on this land for thousands of years. They offer a step toward reintegrating highways into the landscape of more-than-human movement.

These days, there's been a hopeful push for including information about wildlife corridors in decisions about where to build new roads. But that shouldn't mean roads can be built anywhere, as long as they include crossings for animals. Humans aren't the only creatures who need escape routes when conditions change or worsen. "A wildlife crossing is like a Band-Aid," National Wildlife Federation researcher Trisha White told the *New York Times*. "The road is like a wound."

A few years ago, Matt and I wanted to host a party called How to Kill a Highway. This wasn't a fantasy of ecoterrorism, but a surprisingly difficult and pertinent problem—our city had announced a plan to decommission the Skyway, an elevated piece of Route 5, which arches more than a hundred feet above the Buffalo harbor. The mayor was taking proposals for what to do with it. Given that highways have been such historical agents of segregation and environmental racism in American cities, what could be done with two lanes of empty throughfare? There were proposals for an observation deck, a greenway with trees and bike lanes, a glassed-in tropical garden. What if, instead, we wondered, this chunk of Route 5 could be a laboratory for highway decomposition—a test track for all the ways of unmaking such a road?

What better to question, says the writer Georges Perec, than the infra-ordinary, "what seems so much a matter of course that we've forgotten its origins." When I drive in suburbia with my mother, she always points out to me how highways facilitate the fragmenting of human habitats, too. Think of the loneliness of suburbs, where you never have to see your neighbors, where the sidewalks have been replaced by parking lots for big-box stores. Of landscapes where you can drive straight from the office parking lot into the mouth of your garage. Or the white-flight highways that ferry people to these suburbs, sickening and dividing the communities they pass through—like the Cross Bronx Expressway, which displaced nearly as many people as the infamous toxic-waste disaster that unfolded at Love Canal.

I often think of the photo of Miss Blacktop and Miss Concrete, an example of highway-lobby theater at its finest. Two women dressed like beauty queens stand with sashes at a 1958 ribbon cutting to open I-94. In between the women, a man looks down with comical gravity, wielding a large pair of cardboard scissors. Among dignitaries and officials, the women beam with their corsages, their circle skirts stiff with tulle. The overpass behind them is decorated with a neat row of American flags. In my mind, the photo smells of asphalt. Fresh road spools into the distance.

When someone's vertical time has fragmented, one substitution Berger offers is the shelter of romantic love. If you leave your home and find someone to share a life with, he argues, you might be able to rebuild a kind of continuity with memory. For my parents, it wasn't proximity that saved them but a brief return to distance— the miles the highway enabled, stitching them both together and apart. My mother likes to say that she knew it was meant to be when they tried reuniting for a holiday visit and realized they had bought each other the same present. I can see them on the couch, wrapping paper between them, peeling away sheets of tissue. And then laughing, because who else besides them would think antique Shaker clothes hangers were romantic, a gift of utopia, the biggest piece of earthly paradise they could afford?

When I sit with my mother days after her surgery, she tells me this story again. Her first cataract has been removed, and a replacement lens safely implanted. Already, she says, if she covers her right eye she can see farther—out to the neighbors' flagpole, to a cardinal across the marsh. And I realize that her kitchen windows have turned outward again, a bit like what Berger writes about his own experience of surgery: "With cataracts, wherever you are, you are, in a certain sense, indoors." I ask my mother if the color of the sky is bluer. She says it's too early to tell.

I wish I'd remembered all the blues that came back to Berger: those that blend with greens and magentas, those that define fish scales and cloudscapes, the horizon blues of a certain hour, "the colour of depth and distance." The dimensional blue of water, when it appears at the end of the road.

When I arrive in Cornwall, I pass the winter river that curves down the front of my father's last postcard. A covered bridge stretches across. A little fresh snow, unplowed in the roads, to make the image romantic. On the back, my father writes that the East Coast is mild and foggy, "but for the rest the sun shone almost constantly. I remember most vividly," he continues, "the vast, empty spaces." Maybe this is all the road offers: the illusion of emptiness, enough to frighten us so that when the car stops, we desire a way out of our loneliness. None of us knows, or would want to know, the terror of a truly empty landscape. It's enough to contemplate the terror of the irretraceable, of not being able to picture the movements of those we love.

Berger writes that when you lose a beloved, "it is as if your person becomes a place, your contours horizons. I live in you then like living in a country," he continues. "You are everywhere. Yet in that country I can never meet you face to face." Walking among his late wife's raspberry canes, Berger knew something about the precarity of trying to document, about absence as a remorseless cross-examiner, a void that wants to swallow what we've kept about someone. Even these short postcard messages are like markings from another passage, a protection against the silence of the trash heap, saved from the unreadable correspondence of the dead.

And how did I get these postcards? They were handed to me at the end of a long, London afternoon, in a back garden that belonged to my father's friend Phyllis. By the door of her house, the same mail slot where the postman delivered my father's messages decades earlier. From where I sat, 1984 looked like a blip against everything that had happened in the years since, as my parents had become closer than ever, as they'd made a home together, as I'd been born, as my father had died, as my mother and I had survived him, and Phyllis had been widowed, too. The sun was sinking toward the ivy, and my mother and I got up to go. As we were leaving, Phyllis pressed a tidy bundle into my hand. *Thought you might want these.* When I turned the first postcard over, the rest unfolded like a fan.

Phyllis, too, was a sociologist—perhaps she understood what she was giving me: unusual traces, the rare gift beyond the vertical grief of the graveyard. In these remnants of my father's journey, I began to read not just the span of the highway but also its memory, to note the crossings, human and animal, that call out our attendance—the *I'm here, I'm here, I'm here* that shares the road as we drive forward, always forward, into the vanishing point.

DATE	AIRPORT	STATE	OPERATOR	AIRCRAFT	SPECIES
2019-08-30	KBUF	NY	PIEDMONT AIRLINES	EMB-145	European starling
2019-08-22	KBUF	NY	ALPHA FLYING INC	PILATUS PC12	American kestrel
2019-08-18	KBUF	NY	PIEDMONT AIRLINES	EMB-145	Killdeer
2019-08-09	KBUF	NY	SOUTHWEST AIRLINES	B-737-700	Unknown bird - medium
2019-08-06	KBUF	NY	JETBLUE AIRWAYS	EMB-190	Barn swallow
2019-07-29	KBUF	NY	AMERICAN AIRLINES	A-319	Barn swallow
2019-07-25	KBUF	NY	COMMUTAIR	EMB-145	Unknown bird
2019-07-21	KBUF	NY	SKYWEST AIRLINES	CRJ900	Hawks
2019-07-21	KBUF	NY	SOUTHWEST AIRLINES	B-737-700	Killdeer
2019-07-18	KBUF	NY	ENDEAVOR AIR	CRJ900	Barn swallow
2019-06-11	KBUF	NY	SOUTHWEST AIRLINES	B-737-800	Cedar waxwing
2019-06-08	KBUF	NY	JETBLUE AIRWAYS	EMB-190	European starling
2019-06-08	KBUF	NY	JETBLUE AIRWAYS	EMB-190	European starling
2019-06-03	KBUF	NY	AMERICAN AIRLINES	A-320	Unknown bird
2019-05-26	KBUF	NY	SOUTHWEST AIRLINES	B-737-800	Unknown bird - small
2019-05-20	KBUF	NY	JETBLUE AIRWAYS	A-320	Killdeer
2019-05-17	KBUF	NY	AMERICAN AIRLINES	B-737-800	Unknown bird
2019-05-17	KBUF	NY	REPUBLIC AIRLINES	EMB-170	Falcons, kestrels, falconets
2019-05-17	KBUF	NY	AMERICAN AIRLINES	B-737	Ring-billed gull
2019-04-27	KBUF	NY	PSA AIRLINES	CRJ900	Unknown bird
2019-04-24	KBUF	NY	UPS AIRLINES	B-767-300	European starling
2019-02-03	KBUF	NY	UNKNOWN	UNKNOWN	Ducks
2018-12-13	KBUF	NY	JETBLUE AIRWAYS	EMB-190	Red fox
2018-12-09	KBUF	NY	SOUTHWEST AIRLINES	B-737-700	Gulls
2018-12-03	KBUF	NY	UNKNOWN	UNKNOWN	Snowy owl
2018-11-10	KBUF	NY	SOUTHEAST AIRLINES	B-737-800	Gulls
2018-10-25	KBUF	NY	UNKNOWN	UNKNOWN	Mourning dove
2018-10-24	KBUF	NY	REPUBLIC AIRLINES	EMB-170	Unknown bird
2018-10-03	KBUF	NY	FRONTIER AIRLINES	A-320	Unknown bird
2018-09-21	KBUF	NY	REPUBLIC AIRLINES	EMB-170	Unknown bird
2018-09-19	KBUF	NY	JETBLUE AIRWAYS	EMB-190	Unknown bird
2018-09-16	KBUF	NY	SOUTHWEST AIRLINES	B-737-700	Unknown bird - medium
2018-09-10	KBUF	NY	SOUTHWEST AIRLINES	B-737-800	American kestrel
2018-09-06	KBUF	NY	COMMUTAIR	EMB-145	Unknown bird - small
2018-08-21	KBUF	NY	BUSINESS	DASSAULT-200	Unknown bird - small
2018-08-20	KBUF	NY	SOUTHWEST AIRLINES	B-737-700	European starling
2018-08-09	KBUF	NY	DELTA AIR LINES	CRJ900	Blackbirds
2018-08-07	KBUF	NY	SOUTHWEST AIRLINES	B-737-700	Unknown bird - small
2018-08-06	KBUF	NY	UNKNOWN	UNKNOWN	Barn swallow
2018-08-05	KBUF	NY	UNKNOWN	UNKNOWN	Barn swallow
2018-08-02	KBUF	NY	ALLEGIANT AIR	A-320	Unknown bird - small
2018-08-01	KBUF	NY	UPS AIRLINES	A-300	Unknown bird
2018-07-31	KBUF	NY	JETBLUE AIRWAYS	A-320	Barn swallow
2018-07-31	KBUF	NY	UPS AIRLINES	A-300	Unknown bird

7

If I'm Lonely

On a February Monday, I woke up at 4 a.m. and made my way to the Buffalo airport to catch my usual flight to Boston. I was always the first one at my building on Mondays, and I unlocked the front door, opened my office, and went to check the mail. Finding nothing in the box, I shuffled out for a coffee and drank it at my desk, waiting for my colleagues to come upstairs. But no one else arrived. No classes began. A gust blew uninterrupted off the river and howled across the air shaft like a child blowing on the mouth of a bottle. At last it dawned on me that I'd flown an unnecessary four hundred miles before breakfast. It was Presidents' Day, a holiday. Everyone else was at home.

Somewhere in the corridor of offices a clock was ticking resolutely forward. A mouse darted under the baseboard, escaping with some morsel into the conduits of her world. I combed through my inbox for something, anything, that could make my presence needed, that could justify the cost of the flight. I sent emails, received autoreplies. The empty building pressed in, provoking small tendrils of panic. I thought about the airport lines I'd waited in, the flocks of shorebirds over the harbor, how I'd rushed myself through their crooked wings to arrive alone in this small room. After an hour, I gave up and admitted it—I had nowhere to be.

I put on my coat and went outside. Gulls circled over the dumpsters behind the dining hall. The wind was dropping and a light snow was settling on the tops of railings and bike racks. As I headed away from campus, I stepped out of my usual routes through campus, out of the rut of my commute. Commonwealth Ave was picking up a little. A low sky closed over the roofs, and the air in my lungs felt solid—as if the gray weight could hold me down. Near the sluice gate where the Charles meets Muddy River, I passed a convent house run by nuns, where I sometimes rented a room—one of the many Spartan places Boston offers to those who need somewhere cheap to stay for the night. Across the street there was a path, which I hoped would lead out of the highway interchanges into the reeds beyond.

A galaxy of ice melt cleared the track under my feet. Before long, the noise of cars receded and I paused, caught between the skeletons of winter allotments and a wall of phragmites. The snow clung to every twig and bramble, to the fluff at the top of each reed. In the clear spaces, I could see a watercourse curving through the banks.

I didn't think much of Boston in those days. What to make of a city whose accent is shouted into a traffic jam, where it takes longer to get somewhere on the T than it does to ride your bike? I couldn't imagine feeling welcomed by it, or at least not for long. I didn't know then how this city had been built on water, how the entirety of the neighborhood where I worked had once been tidal marshes and creeks. Mudflats like the one I lived on as a child, where the sea drained away and returned, bringing fish and horseshoe crabs.

In fact, the name Back Bay is literal—in the 1800s, the blocks of this neighborhood expanded into the water, filling an entire cove of salt grasses. If I felt unsteady there, well, I wasn't entirely on dry land. Boston Common was once on the shoreline, overlooking the estuary. All these roads, these apartment towers of student housing, these 7-Elevens and tanning salons, all this had once been underwater at high tide. The public library was once a fishing ground, a site where, for more than two hundred generations, the Massachusett built fishweirs, piling their boats with the spring catch. What is now Beacon Street was a narrow causeway, the first road built across the mouth of the bay.

It's not uncommon for American cities to be built on filled land, but over the centuries, Boston has changed its coastline much more radically than most. Historian Nancy Seasholes points out that the original peninsula the settlers occupied was small, and the townspeople were reluctant to move to the adjacent marshland. For them, it was easier to fill the shallow water surrounding the spit. Throughout the nineteenth and into the twentieth century, Bostonians made land for new railways and roads and shipping and aviation, for the expansion of neighborhoods, and, most significantly, to bury areas they had polluted.

In total, landmaking projects in the city have created over five thousand acres (some two thousand city blocks) since white settlers colonized the area in 1630. Interventions in the landscape were often most extreme in the central parts of the city—where the original area of downtown was only a narrow peninsula. The entirety of Back Bay is fill, a cove narrowed over time by real estate investors who were creating land they could develop. According to geographer Garrett Dash Nelson, these projects were another way of "making water into gold." "The legacy of landmaking," he writes, "coupled with the continued financial value of urban space means that a huge amount of Boston's wealth—as well as the tax revenue that's generated from property assessment—rests literally on invented property."

The filling of Back Bay began with a dam to contain the power of the tide. When the construction was complete, an 1850s dignitary described the wondrous transformation of the city as a fist that had been allowed to open—a left fist, with bridges for spreading fingers. The dam across Back Bay was the thumb—a key piece of infrastructure to harness the flow of water and power industrial mills. But you could also call it a widening handspan across the marsh, a giant palm opened and waiting to be greased.

Unfortunately for the developers, Back Bay landmaking concentrated shit as well as wealth. While development expanded in the nineteenth century, bringing the shore closer to the dam, Back Bay became known for two things. It was a growing upper-middle-class neighborhood in a city that desperately needed more housing. And it was a pool of raw sewage and filth that became fouler as development filled in the bay. The problem had several causes. For decades, residents had simply piped their sewage into the closest water source, and the flow was increasing as houses adopted indoor plumbing. Inland neighborhoods used the two creeks that emptied into the bay as sewers, effectively catching all this runoff into one giant tidal cesspool. And the way to deal with a stinking mud pit next door was often to cover it with "clean" fill like gravel, making it into land, and further shrinking the dammed basin. All these methods meant that more sewage and runoff were being piped into smaller waterways, making them increasingly toxic and prone to flooding.

One observer noted in 1849 that the pollution of Back Bay was so bad it had become almost diabolical: "A greenish scum, many yards wide, stretches along the shores of the basin . . . the surface of the water beyond is seen bubbling like a cauldron with the noxious gases that are exploding from the corrupting mass below."

By the second half of the nineteenth century, it was clear that between the thumb of the dam and the shoreline, Boston landmakers had precipitated the creation of a discarded landscape, a sacrifice zone where not even bivalves would live.

Even today, walking through Boston's streets evokes a kind of aloofness—a self-protectiveness that polices the city's separation from its water. The town houses themselves turn away from the river, with their window boxes street-side and their garbage cans facing the Charles. When I stepped into the reeds that winter morning, I felt something emerging—a longing I'd suppressed, startled out of its shell by the sudden hush of these surroundings.

The water curled and eddied here; the ground was soft. I could begin to imagine its depth and receptivity, snowmelt slowly filling the prints that dotted the ground, easing them back into the earth. And I remembered something Matt had said, about the last time he'd walked to work in Ann Arbor before leaving, how he'd imagined all his previous selves on that particular route, like one long exposure dragged across film, and while he'd walked that path, it had kept him company; it had been a kind of continuity. During my years of flying, I didn't know if it was wise to give in and let myself be shaped by the commuter routes I traveled, the ephemeral transits through the air that fed the unsteady, quixotic parts of me. Safer, I thought, to stay in sharp compartments—home, job—than in the murk of constant departure, moving on flight paths of untouchable blue. The more I traveled, the more I began to see the time in the air as one long postponement—coming between me and some kind of arrival I kept deferring, each time I counted on one hand the days between touchdown and take-off. It was still early, not even ten, and the sun had burned only a little way through the clouds. But I'd been awake for almost seven hours, and I could feel the gulf of tiredness lapping on the other side of the caffeine.

When the poet Adrienne Rich lived in Boston, she wrote that she was sleepwalking—long days of caring for her young children, followed by the "ludicrous" dinner parties of Harvard Square. In this city, she, too, had held herself apart. Buried under the surface of care and obligation, she'd lived through part of the litany in her poem "Song" from *Diving into the Wreck*: "If I'm lonely," go the famous lines, " / it must be the loneliness / of waking first, of breathing / dawn's first cold breath on the city." There's something abandoned in this stanza—the silence of being awake when no one else wants to be. To have a moment alone with your true self, sometimes you have to also admit loneliness. And yet the taste of the air is still real, perhaps even promising.

Walking by the water, I thought about Rich as I watched my small clouds of breath unfurling. Parts of the bank had frozen, leaving promontories of ice that darkened where they touched deeper channels. The pace of the current, the joggers, even the squirrels felt unhurried. I hadn't expected to let my guard down here, but the air was full of the soft clicks of reeds. Sparrows bobbed in the thicket and cardinals searched for berries. Half sinking into the mud, I followed a neat row of tracks as they approached the waterline, unsure if they belonged to a dog or a fox. Slowly I realized this place wasn't a park at all but the Fens—a wetland like the winter marshes I'd grown up with, minus the traces of salt.

The year Boston's commissioners approached the landscape architect Frederick Law Olmsted about Back Bay, their tails were between their legs. They had acquired a hundred unwieldy acres of polluted mudflats, and the design contest they'd just sponsored had failed to generate a plan. The public was still complaining about the water in the cove, which was so filthy that few fish swam there. Maybe the area could be cleaned up and become a green space, the commissioners thought, with a concrete basin where the public could paddle. But Olmsted refused to call the area a park, despite the dismay this provoked in his clients. And he didn't want to build a basin either. For him, this project was not a work of art but an "improvement," located on a place so degraded and vile, and so in need of amendment, that it would be unwise to raise the public's expectations. "If the state of Massachusetts had been hunted over," Olmsted wrote, "a space combining more disadvantages for a park could not have been found." He scoffed that "even eels could not live in it."

Yet even more than "park," "improvement" was a grandiose, biblical word. It had come to the field of landscape architecture from the earliest days of European settlement, and it still carried traces of the colonial enterprise—the providential grace the Europeans bargained on when they arrived in America to clumsily till the "wilderness." A word used to justify the privatization of property and the stealing of Indigenous land. But what did it mean to improve the mess that European settlers had left? The project itself could not have been less glamorous. The acres the city commissioners had sourced were really just the dregs left over from landmaking. A channel of "flowing mud," too deep, in parts, to fill for profit. It was rife with sewage and runoff from streets and mills. It stank so badly in the summer that people avoided it, afraid to inhale the air. And when high tide coincided with heavy rains, it flooded, sending shit and effluvia into neighboring streets.

Olmsted's reaction to the problem was to ask if he could build a salt marsh. In 1879, this request was highly unusual. Landscape architects had a history of designing formal parks with picturesque fountains or grand vistas of pastoral elegance. They "civilized" domestic landscapes into charming pleasure grounds for people, especially wealthy people. One of the best examples of this design tradition was the ha-ha, a narrow earthen ditch with raised banks, named after the aristocratic burst of laughter or surprise it was designed to provoke. Unlike fences, which might disrupt the view, ha-has were invisible from the windows of a manor, and they kept livestock (and their minders) at a picturesque distance from country estates. When landscape architects thought of wilderness in that era, it was often the "unspoiled" kind that would be attributed to many national parks, where Indigenous and Black inhabitants were forcibly removed to make space for game hunters and tourists, undermining long traditions of coexistence, mutual benefit, and collaboration with other species. This separation played into the idea of nature as a vista to visit, creating the illusion that to be authentic, it had to be free of the long-term presence of people. Olmsted himself was not entirely exempt from this pattern. Though he ultimately became an abolitionist after traveling through the American South, he also helped to design Central Park after New York City commissioners razed Seneca Village, clearing land and dispossessing settlements of free Blacks and immigrants through eminent domain.

In Olmsted's lifetime, marshes, swamps, and estuaries offered an opportunity for a different model, since they'd already been discarded from European ideas of the majestic sublime. Though this Boston marsh might not offer dramatic vistas, it could be an "urban wild" before its time, integrated into a city neighborhood. On the site of the original basin, he would create a tidal creek's meander—through clumps of sedge and salt grass, restoring the flow between the Charles River and Back Bay, and diverting the worst of the pollution into sewers and underground culverts. This work would require filling and dredging to make the course of the channel, but to the untrained eye, the result wouldn't look man-made. Unlike a park, the meadow of marsh grass wasn't intended for playgrounds or athletic fields. The curving waterway would prevent surf and erosion, and the sloped banks would minimize flooding.

For a long time, I wondered how Olmsted's experience might have led him to choose this plan. Yet there was a time in his life that's now glossed over, a time before he was famous, when he was nearly thirty and with few prospects, trying to farm potatoes on a piece of land his father had bought him in Guilford, Connecticut. His acres led down to Long Island Sound, on the same peninsula of wetland and granite outcroppings where I searched for horseshoe crabs as a child. Olmsted left after less than two years, but perhaps this landscape somehow impressed itself on him, with its long creek beds curving through meadows of spartina, slow waterways where a person can feel enveloped as they drift.

In Boston, Olmsted toyed with names like "The Sea Glades" and "Sedgeglade," before settling on "the Back Bay Fens." Rather than covering the area, he would bring "the wild," whatever it meant, to the city-dwellers, and to those who could not travel. But he wasn't actually bringing a new ecosystem into the city as an environmental fix. He was re-creating the very habitat that had been eclipsed by development—recognizing the ecologically protective value of marshland at a time when others viewed such landscapes as pestilential and worthless. To preserve a marsh was one thing, but to actually build one was unheard-of—a rare decision to collaborate with the ecology and history of the place. The Fens provided a remediation of this landscape that was tidy enough for people to forget that anyone had intervened at all. "The best result that can be hoped for," Olmsted writes,

> is that after trees have grown and nature has in various ways not to be minutely anticipated come to our aid, and in effect adopted and given a truly natural character to the details of the salt creek and salt marsh elements, it will appear that there is nothing artificial about the affair except the roads and bridges required for convenience, but that the city has grown up about the locality leaving all within its boundaries in an undisturbed natural state.

Today, this strip of land presents as a slice of "preserved nature" rather than a built ecosystem. But aren't there drawbacks to overlooking what people have had to restore? It seems dangerous to forget that a place was once so desolate that people avoided the area and remarked that not even clams and eels could survive. Olmsted tried to be such an effective surgeon that he left no visible scar. Which meant that those who followed, who didn't see the before and after, lost touch with the changes wrought by the restoration. Landscape architect Anne Whiston Spirn writes that in the case of the Fens, "the persistent mental opposition of nature and city gradually eroded the memory of Olmsted's contribution."

Building a wetland requires cooperation between species in a way that erases the false categories of wild and tame, civilized and desolate. And to insist on nature as if it cannot be made is to miss what's beautiful about the Fens. At a time when Back Bay developers were battling to bury the estuary and keep the water away, the Fens represent a refusal to fight. Though they aren't advertised this way, their meander is like a monument to Boston's estuarial ecosystem—the site of an unlikely truce.

As the sun crested the trees into a fuzzy noon, I doubled back through the plots of the Fenway Victory Gardens, one of the gentler marks a war can leave on the landscape of the home front. As the paths narrowed away from the water, I could see that people had come by to visit their allotments, even on a late-winter day. When I pulled out my phone to check the map, I found photos of the growing season—pink marshmallows big as a handspan, and great blue herons standing in the ornamental pools. In the winter quiet, there were still signs of human hospitality to wildlife. Birdhouses bobbed on their branches, stalks of milkweed had winnowed down to their pods. Between the homespun fences of scrap wood and chicken wire, the brittle seed heads of coneflowers had long since been picked over by migrating finches. The snow dripped from the bones of the garden, leaving dark circles where it touched the dirt.

I sat for a bit on a plastic chair someone had left in the open, feeling the chill soak into the back of my coat. I wanted, in that moment, to have been the person who left this seat, to have tended this allotment, to have pressed my hands into its soil. These were old trees, old gardens, and I knew the earth beneath them would be full of long-developed networks of fungi, tiny filaments running through the soil, mycelia guided by the attraction of one filament tip to another, a process called homing. Why did I remember these things when I'd never actually planted a garden? When I'd never lived anywhere long enough? I waited for the feeling to pass, but it didn't.

I kept finding places I could love just as I was leaving. The soft curves of the riverbank, the allotments, the many times someone had planted seeds here and they were stolen by some other creature—all these small chances and surprises that make up the real privilege of knowing a place, of rootedness, of being able to stay. I wished I could show Matt this garden, that we could wait together for it to green and loosen, but the best I could do was braid his absence through the reeds and make a space of concurrent hunger—for that one person, for this evolving world.

"Longing is never over. . . . ," the poet Alina Ştefănescu says. "It's like loitering. It is an intellectual sauntering. It's just agreeing, for a minute, to feel something." She's talking about the Romanian word dor, which isn't easy to describe in English—the pain of deep longing, often for someone or somewhere you love. For Ştefănescu, there's power in language that can map that ache onto both people and places—that can bind the feelings that seep in when we let ourselves saunter, when we allow ourselves to inhabit the desire to simply linger over a place together, even a remembered or invented place.

A posted placard informed me that though these gardens were not part of the original plan for the Fens, they span more than seven acres, attracting bugs and bird life. I saw flyers asking gardeners to participate in community science surveys of insect biodiversity, and materials advertising that these allotments have grown food and flowers for more than 475 people from every neighborhood in Boston. Walking among these plots, I thought about what it might mean to garden on the site of a scar, to eat the fruit of that liminal space.

I wanted to stay, but the day was moving, and I was just a commuter, a passenger, a ghost. At last, I stood up from the chair, startling a gray squirrel as it dug for something it had cached in the dirt. His tail flicked three times—*what, what, what*—the backward curve of a question mark. I admired his alertness. I left the gardens and followed the path.

It's often taken for granted, but Olmsted's park system was inadvertently responsible for inviting both marshlands and squirrels back into Boston. You wouldn't guess it now, but in the 1600s and 1700s, settlers had decimated the population of eastern gray squirrels, to the point that they disappeared from most northeastern settlements. As the colonists cut down forests for timber and firewood, they destroyed squirrel habitats, while also killing tens of millions of individual animals. By the time the Declaration of Independence was written, there were so few squirrels in the wild that they had become exotic pets. And as pets, squirrels had permission to enter the human-made ecosystems of cities, which were increasingly devoid of wildlife—and therefore of squirrel predators.

Though many tourists come to Boston seeking colonial history, they often don't know how the gray squirrel was nearly eradicated by early settlers, and how their descendants began to miss the sounds of small paws rustling through the trees. In 1772, Benjamin Franklin wrote an elegy for a pet squirrel, which is, in the history of human-creature relations, a very perplexing and suggestive document. "He should not go," Franklin begins, "without an Elegy or an Epitaph. Let us give him one in the monumental Stile and Measure, which being neither Prose nor Verse, is perhaps the properest for Grief; since to use common Language would look as

if we were not affected, and to make Rhimes would seem Trifling in
Sorrow." He continues:

> Alas! poor *Mungo*!
> Happy wert thou, hadst thou known
> Thy own Felicity!
> Remote from the fierce Bald-Eagle,
> Tyrant of thy native Woods,
> Thou hadst nought to fear from his piercing Talons;
> Nor from the murdering Gun
> Of the thoughtless Sportsman.

Leaving off the rhymes to better chronicle grief for a squirrel! Or
to make that grief apparent in "monumental Stile." It makes you
wonder what this elegy is really about. Here the "Bald-Eagle" and
the human hunter are hand in hand, in a partnership of predatory
power. In fact, when the bald eagle became the national bird years
later, Franklin protested: "I wish the bald eagle had not been chosen
as the representative of our country. He is a bird of bad moral character. . . . like those among men who live by sharping and robbing."
Absurd as all this is, there's something resonant about it. The tyrant
of the "native Woods" becomes the emblem of a human country that
eradicates its forests. Though the human is portrayed as thoughtless
rather than tyrannical, there's a fair amount of projection there. And
in any case, the results, for the squirrel, are the same.

Within a hundred years of this elegy, the "Felicity" that Mungo enjoyed began to reach urban squirrel populations at large. Parks and
city commons began to release pairs of pet squirrels, but they were
not expected to survive on their own. Occupying a status between
civic ward and endangered species, squirrels in the mid-to-late
1800s were fed and housed at the expense of the city commissioners. Ordinary citizens fed them, too, sustaining them through
winters in parks where there weren't enough trees to nourish and
house them. Boston Common was one such place. As historian

Etienne Benson writes, early environmentalists perceived squirrels as a species that had been decimated by the way the settlers treated forested landscapes, and that "the tameness of the squirrels of the Common was a foretaste of the rewards to be expected when man moderated his destructive behavior toward nature."

The relationship was transactional: by showing clemency toward squirrels, Bostonians could disprove their connections to many forms of socialized cruelty. As vehicles of human conscience-clearing, squirrels opened the floodgates for early attempts to assuage the lack of wildlife in city parks. Urban squirrels, with their anthropomorphized gratitude, offered absolution through feeding. But as Benson points out, the food was often nutritionally poor or impossible to bury in caches to preserve it through the winter. Which meant that when humans didn't show up, the creatures went hungry.

Luckily for the squirrels, Olmsted's landscapes changed the ways other species could survive in urban spaces that weren't designed for them. For one thing, he brought in clusters of trees, and connected his projects with tree-lined parkways, which were designed to boost real estate values. Yet these corridors also gave arboreal wildlife a conduit between isolated green spaces. "The conditions of existence for squirrels in American cities improved significantly from the 1870s onward . . . ," Benson writes. "Compared with public squares, commons, and town greens, Olmstedian landscape parks provided much larger and more suitable habitats for squirrels, while also bolstering the justification for introducing and maintaining them." Rather than being subjects of public charity and vehicles for the absolution of eco-guilt, landscape parks gave eastern grays a viable habitat where they could be *squirrels*.

What was uncommon can reappear, and what was common can recede and vanish. As environmental historian Peter Alagona writes, "Eastern grays were among the first wild animals to return to the hearts of American cities, but they would not be the last."

In 2008, elementary school students, artists, and members of the Massachusett Tribe built a weir on Boston Common to catch the memory of fish. It was May—the season of spring herring runs, when Indigenous Americans would build a woven mesh of sticks along the tide line in the marshlands that became Back Bay. As the water returned, the weir would contain the catch, making for an abundant harvest. As they put it: "We continue to survive as Massachusett people because we have retained the oral tradition of storytelling just as our ancestors did. This tradition passes on the Massachusett view of how our world works, our relationship with all of nature and why things are the way they are." In a city rife with colonial history, the Ancient Fishweir Project was designed to push back at forgetting, to focus on how the Massachusett have cared for and cultivated this landscape over millennia—before 1630, and into the future.

The project began with a strange fact about the Green Line T station at Boylston Street, where I used to race down the platform, sweating in my heavy coat. In 1913, while workers were digging the tunnels for trains, they stumbled on five-thousand-year-old fragments of fishweirs that had been staked into the mud. Suddenly, with the coming and going of trains, I could imagine the cyclical return of herring, their silver sides flashing in the tunnel, muscling alongside the T. Beyond identifying a fishweir or updating a plaque in a train station, these are sites whose layered stories require deep, sustained responses. Architectural historian Mark Jarzombek has argued for emphasizing "the ambiguity and incompletion of these locations so as to allow us, perhaps, to imagine a new form of citizen landscape altogether."

In the video from that day on the Common, kids run around with sticks, adding them to thicken the structure that ripples across the lawn like a giant undulating nest. They're wearing big T-shirts slipped over their jackets, emblazoned with the words *Weir Here.* You can listen to Gill Solomon, Sac'hem of the Massachusett Tribe at Ponkapoag, speak to the group of children, asking them to tell their friends about what they built, asking them to return next year and continue the cycle. His voice is soft and sure, and at times it carries the hard *a* of a Boston accent. He's talking about duration, about what forever can outlast.

✎

Given the choice between a monument and an ecosystem, most people these days would pick the ecosystem itself. As a restored replica of Boston's marshlands, and as a way to hide a problem developers had created, the Fens weren't designed to alter the forces that had buried the city's mudflats in the first place. Only fifteen years after the Fens were finished, the city built a new dam across the Charles River to keep the tide out of the estuary. What was salt became freshwater, and many of the plants Olmsted had selected died off, including much of the grass and sedge. And over time, phragmites took hold, narrowing the watercourse further. As Boston developers lived alongside the Fens and forgot their origin, they also began to think of them as extraneous land that could be filled exactly the same way they'd filled the landscape the Fens mimicked.

The expediencies of war that brought gardeners into the Fens morphed into the demands of people who wanted to raze both allotments and marsh for a hospital, a stadium, and at worst, a parking lot. As one chair of the Massachusetts Turnpike Authority put it, the Victory Gardens were a "waste of space." The allotment organizers protested, asking to keep their beds and trellises, their sleepy benches visited by bees. A place not just to live on the soil of the city but to touch it. Though they were not to the letter of the original plan, the allotments represented a refusal to stop lingering in the landscape the Fens created. And this refusal has protected both garden and wetland from becoming a lake of asphalt.

Despite the visibility of Olmsted's parks in Boston, part of this land-scape did get buried. In 1950, around the same time Logan airport was expanding toward Wood Island, the Sears Roebuck Company persuaded the city to allow a parking lot to be built over one end of the Fens—right where the marsh meets Muddy River, where there were no gardeners to protect it. The flow of water was diverted into culverts, and a whole section of the wetland disappeared for several decades under concrete and cars.

Rivers, though, have a way of making themselves remembered. In 1996, three days of heavy rain fell, and the Fens flooded, as they had in the days before their improvement. Basements in Brookline and Back Bay filled with water, and the Kenmore T station was in-undated. In 1998, the same thing happened again. It turned out that the culverts under the parking lot were too small to handle the flow. At the beginning of the new millennium, Boston and the Army Corps of Engineers agreed to dredge the Fens, removing the phragmites and sending polluted sediment that had collected in their roots to a dump for hazardous waste. They also decided to resize the culverts, and ultimately to "daylight" the river where it passes under the shadow of a long-bankrupt Sears.

The Fens were unburied in part because of their slipperiness, their duality. Their persistence has to do with the fact that their design not only re-created a marsh—it also eased infrastructure problems that were difficult to solve. Beyond the Fens, Olmsted talked the city engineer into planning for Muddy River, so he could reme-diate the water before it entered the channel. Rather than con-taining the pollution upstream (which would have meant merely moving the sacrifice zone), he argued successfully to extend his project further. Because the marsh is also a sanitation scheme, it's harder to pave over.

When so many places need to be remediated, it's worth thinking about spaces like the Fens that are not less vital because they were never meant to be pristine. Through the messy layers of restoring a restoration, the Fens persist as a space where it's possible to be in dialogue with the past of these mudflats and creeks. As they evolve beyond their original design, they are still hospitable to plants and insects and squirrels and people—they speak to anyone who would like to be a citizen of longing for repair.

In the world of the winter marsh, it had once again begun to snow. The day was turning on its axis, bruising into afternoon. Under my coat, my shoulders tensed from the cold. I'd reached the lawn in front of the Isabella Stewart Gardner Museum, and I crossed under the glass facade, shaking the weather from my hair. At the ticket counter, I paid the entrance fee and passed into the incongruous warmth of what was once another woman's home.

After the Fens were built, one of the first people to buy land next to the marsh was Isabella Stewart Gardner—an art collector and millionaire who had just lost her husband. In the wake of his sudden absence, she fashioned a home for herself at the edge of the wetland, a Venetian palazzo filled with treasures that she immortalized at great expense, like an installation artist before her time. When she started building, in 1899, there wasn't much else around—in photos you can see the stark outline of the mansion, surrounded by half-built marshes. These days a Venetian palace doesn't seem so out of place in the Fenway, where the land still vies with water, where houses shift and sink on their pilings. To her contemporaries it was shocking—a recently widowed woman going every day to check on her construction site in the middle of a swamp. But by all accounts, she enjoyed it. She even participated in the construction process, taking a hatchet to some ceiling beams when they arrived insufficiently distressed. And terrorizing her architect, whose name (though he bore no relation to the department store) was Sears.

Rather than daylighting a river, Sears opened the center of Isabella's home with a landscaped courtyard, where jasmine and cycads grow. Because Isabella left her house to the city as a museum, you can still visit these corridors that open onto porticoes of light. On that Monday in February, couples were lounging on the stone benches, some holding hands, some on what looked like first dates. I walked around under the colonnaded arches, thinking of Matt's hands on the steering wheel in the dark of early morning. The shadows of tree ferns passed across my face. I climbed to an upper floor, where a woman smiled at me as she moved away from a window, letting me take a turn. This garden, too, had a generosity that felt collaborative, and as I looked at the green fronds growing even in the depths of a Boston winter, I wanted to believe that a place is not something dwelled in but something created together—through the hard fact of entanglement with other beings, by the life's work of kinship and hospitable proximity.

Down in the courtyard, a mosaic marked the house's heart. Among the arabesques of tile, I could just make out a face—Medusa, with her serpentine hair, the only mortal Gorgon, whose blood mixed with the sea and became reefs of messy, symbiotic life. In Donna Haraway's version, Medusa is a warrior, an ecological icon. Someone who could "heighten our chances for dashing the twenty-first-century ships of the Heroes on a living coral reef instead of allowing them to suck the last drop of fossil flesh out of dead rock." But here, in the middle of this palace, Medusa looked younger, and softer. She had wings in her hair among the snakes. Her gaze was wary—the eyeshine of a creature—but from the window where I stood, her mouth crooked upward with kindness, a beatific vulnerability, almost like she was smiling. And beneath her face, the ground made from polluted tides, all the trouble of that fill and its erasures, the ways water follows its law. As if the Gorgon had anchored this palace in loss and its transmutable longing—raw and hungry and listening into the wind.

When I left the museum, I loitered for a moment by the cattails and brambles. At the edge of the marsh, pools of water scattered over a flooded field like pockets of desires, surfacing. Sparrows flew out of the thicket around me, but when I stood still for a moment, they returned. I watched them advancing twig by twig through the brush, with bright, effortless movements, their hollow bones built for weightlessness, for filling their bodies with air. The wind rose, touching my face, and I wondered if some part of that gust had once been inside the bones of a sparrow. And I knew, then, that I would quit my commute. That this wandering day had eased the split of a deep two-body problem—between the person and the passenger in me.

8

The Echo

We park and enter from the west, past a pair of concrete cylinders meant to deter traffic. They crumble in the street, adorned with a pack of fluorescent reflectors. I'm still not sure what kind of marker I expected. It's spring. Almost bucolic. Last season's milkweed still standing in the field.

Incursions of grasses and trees soften the edges of the road, where some of the storm drains have lost their grates. But it doesn't matter. The holes are plugged anyway, with what looks like rubble. Dry fire hydrants gape, their outlets broken open. In meadows where the roads have vanished, rows of dead streetlights tilt like the lures of deep-sea fish. It must be bathysmal here at night—just voices and the ends of cigarettes, trembling in the dark.

As we study the traces of a driveway, screams begin to echo over the empty fields. The cries of children. We freeze until we realize they're cheering—across the street from the containment area, the last inning has just ended. It's Little League day at the baseball diamond where the 93rd Street School used to be.

Matt follows me down what remains of the block. It occurs to me that we're not the first couple to research the neighborhood, to walk around these streets on a spring afternoon. If we'd arrived fifty years earlier, we might have seen real estate brokers with families trailing along behind, anxious and acquisitive, debating about which place to rent or buy. Split-level versus ranch. A new dishwasher. An extra freezer in the garage. All vanished. Every so often, a former cul-de-sac appears, making a round clearing in the brush. As we look up, a man emerges from around the bend, walking a three-legged dog. He doesn't greet us. I can see the clustered roofline of a senior center and the faint shimmer of a chain-link fence. Small signs warn people to pick up after their pets. Nothing else is posted. No indication of what this place is or of what happened here. Because this is Love Canal, the cradle of the Superfund. With few exceptions, the buildings where people lived have been demolished.

As we move east, toxicity concentrates. The streets become narrow and tree-lined, with mature crowns hollowed out to accommodate the supremacy of wires. Someone has taken advantage of the emptiness and dumped a couch by the road, next to a mattress with springs poking through the quilted top. Grass grows beneath the cushions. This side of the landscape is dotted with a handful of houses, heaps of broken concrete, and fenced-off areas where backhoes and trailers park. We pass the gravel lot of an asphalt contractor and a truck branded *Patriot Lawn & Land Beautification, Inc.*

Only one place looks occupied—a tiny bungalow with an aggressively large *Home Sweet Home* sign. Plastic flowers. American flags. After many warnings that we are on camera, we're unsettled, unable to spot the cameras themselves. There's a patch of the grid that has disappeared entirely—the former streets simply dead-end into stubs at the fence. Robins lift, red feathers flashing into a stand of trees.

On our second lap, Matt and I find the gate to the area we've been circling. An emergency number with a Buffalo area code is posted next to the intercom. If you didn't already know what's inside, you'd struggle to imagine the emergency. The *Dangerous Area, Hazardous Waste* signs have been replaced with *Private Property. Keep Out* has become *No Trespassing*, or *Authorization Required*. Beyond the fence lie seventy acres of smooth, grassy rise, yellowed by dandelions— what was once the dump itself, plus the first two rings of houses built around it, the first to be torn down. As I watch, a barn swallow dips over the fence and across the containment area, unconstrained by the official line between habitable and not.

That divide has never felt looser, flimsier, than it does in the sunlight, as we look through the fence at a space that has been declared off-limits in perpetuity. Among the myths and weeds and rumors, the carcinogens and liver enzymes, the myriad and multiplying casualties, there's one fundamental fact: unlike the Fens, Love Canal hasn't been restored, only isolated. And yet people still live next door.

When Matt and I began to think about moving to Buffalo, the Canal and the waterfalls were the only nearby landmarks I knew. From our apartment in Providence, I oriented myself by looking at a map of the Niagara River, winding along the Canadian border toward the Falls. Then I looked up the distance—only fourteen miles—between Buffalo and Love Canal. At the back of all this was a question I couldn't articulate. Something about how to fathom those miles, or how far the ripples of William Love's story stretched.

By the time we moved, Love Canal had been taken off the Superfund list. I'd never been particularly careful about environmental toxins, but I did wonder if it might be better to live somewhere that had been remediated, where the scars weren't as fresh. I believed in the logic of monitoring wells and extra filtration tanks, in the science of habitability decisions and parts per billion. I thought that maybe the long legacy of pollution in Western New York might mean that the landscape had at least partially healed. Now I know better than to pass judgment on the safety of these places—I can only read their traces and surfacing signs, like an archaeologist where it isn't wise to dig.

We arrived in 2018, when Matt took a job at the state university. Before that, I had visited the city exactly once, flying into Buffalo Niagara International Airport for forty-eight hours under sleeting late-March skies. It was Easter weekend, overlapping with Passover. Matt had just been offered the job, and his future colleagues invited us to join their seder. As we knocked and waited on their doorstep, I saw two five-gallon glass jugs on the stoop. It meant, of course, that they must get their drinking water delivered—they didn't trust their tap. I was mulling the implications when their young son opened the door and asked us if we were the ghost of Elijah, come for his cup of wine.

At first, I thought the history of toxicity in Western New York began with the factories, but no—it really begins with water: its power, and its hidden channels that meander through the earth. Abundant, fast-flowing water drew manufacturing to the area along the river that poured through the gorge between Great Lakes. In old photographs, you can see the millraces churning down the cliffs where factories perched, making paper, flour, aluminum. When William T. Love arrived in 1892, he was an unproved industrialist who wanted to dig an eleven-mile-long canal between the upper and lower Niagara River to generate electricity for businesses. And beyond the canal, he would build a place where both workers and captains of industry could live. He called this grand metropolis Model City, and claimed it would house hundreds of thousands of people between Lake Ontario and the Tuscarora Nation. In Model City, the rhetoric was progressive: streets would be laid out in a tidy grid, alcohol would be forbidden, and everyone would get rich under bright streetlamps beneath the unpolluted sky.

Predictably, things did not work out as planned. As Love prepared to break ground for his canal, he was confronted with the Panic of 1893. The stock market crashed, and a play called *The War of Wealth* appeared on Broadway, dramatizing flailing investors and a run on a bank that somehow ended with the bricks of the vault exploding across the stage. While the play was a success, Love's canal went bankrupt. Less than a mile of it was ever dug. Model City, New York, still exists, but only as a name on a map. Its streets are abandoned, except for strange dump trucks that arrive by night.

In 1941, much of the land at Model City was requisitioned by the Department of Defense to build the Lake Ontario Ordnance Works, a manufacturing plant for TNT. Though the initial facility was decommissioned after less than a year, residues from TNT production were buried and dumped around the site. Then 1,500 acres were transferred to the Manhattan Engineer District. Starting in the forties, this area was used, as the Army Corps of Engineers bluntly puts it, for the "storage of radioactive materials during the development of the atomic bomb."

Left to its own devices, Love's story might have ended there and been forgotten. The sides of the canal might have softened and eroded, collapsing back into the earth. The half-lives of radioactive ions might have quietly unfolded in the woods. But that timeline wasn't to be. Just up the road, at the nearby Hooker Chemical Company, business was booming. Its founder, Elon Hooker, made a fortune manufacturing chemicals for tanning, gasoline, and lubricants, among other things. During the First World War, Hooker made so much thionyl chloride that he was christened "the 'Poison Gas King' of America."

When the Second World War approached, Hooker Chemical once again prepared for the wartime bump in demand. Disposing of waste was a problem, especially as the military awarded huge contracts to companies across Erie and Niagara Counties. Writer Ginger Strand reports that at the height of production, some manufacturers were desperate enough to pay individual workers fifty dollars apiece to take home a drum of waste and make it disappear. Dumps opened overnight. And the long trench of Love's canal was just up the road.

In 1942, Hooker got permission to begin using it as a site for disposing of chemicals and residues from the factories. In a single decade, the company dumped twenty-two thousand tons of chemicals into the canal. According to the writer Keith O'Brien, Hooker stationed an employee at the edge with a hose in case the chaotic mix of leaking drums caused a reaction and caught fire. Though water is not always the best way to quench a chemical burn.

Eventually, a few people at Hooker began to worry. The city of Niagara Falls was expanding, and the neighborhood was becoming more residential as young families chased the fantasy of postwar suburban life. In the forties, the Griffon Manor housing project was built right next to the canal. Families who lived there gardened alongside it. Though the dump had begun in a relatively rural area, by 1950 it was not so sparsely populated. Kids played in the ditches at the edge of the water. And in 1952, the school board offered to buy the land from Hooker to build a new elementary school.

Initially, the company declined the offer—but they were weighing competing forces. On the one hand, the land was dangerous. On the other hand, the school board had given them an advantageous chance to get rid of their liability. In the end, Hooker capped the dump and sold the land to the Board of Education for a dollar. In a clause that would become crucial, the company disclosed the presence of "waste products" and relinquished any future responsibility for hazards they might cause. As sociologist Adeline Levine writes, "The day of reckoning was deferrable, with the impact and responsibility to be borne by someone else."

For over twenty years, residents thought of it as a safe neighborhood, a place where even if you weren't wealthy, you could buy a first home. The day of reckoning was deferrable. The dump uneasily slept.

❧

Our preparations for moving to Buffalo consisted of renting a yellow cottage from a friend of a friend and watching a series of vlogs by a YouTuber couple who had moved to Buffalo from New York City. Late at night, in the midst of our moving boxes, we watched as they kayaked on Lake Erie, drove up to Lewiston for hikes by the river, donned ponchos under the spray of the falls, or installed raised beds in the backyard of their gingerbreaded Victorian. (Activities all subsidized by Visit Buffalo Niagara, the tourist board whose ads punctuated these wholesome scenes.) It seems a little naive now, like clickbait for gentrifiers. But at the time, Matt and I watched closely, exchanging glances each time the camera lingered on someplace we hoped we could love. *Keep Buffalo a Secret*, a downtown mural read, and we thought that maybe, if we were lucky, someone would let us in on it.

As we scrolled backward in time through their videos, we reached the one where they live streamed their move, driving a truck through New York State at dawn. As they pull into Buffalo, it starts snowing in early April and one of them laughs and says, *What have we done.* Then the frame cuts out and the more upbeat of the two pans around their new place. *The snow melted like a bad dream*, he says.

❧

The winter of 1976 to 1977 was one of the harshest in Buffalo's history. Over sixty inches of snow fell in both December and January. The drifts piled up on the ice until a blizzard on January 28 blew all that snow off the lake and into the city. The whiteout lasted thirteen hours. Forecasters called it a two-hundred-year weather event, one that's become so cliché, and so synonymous with Buffalo, that there was even a poster about it at the airport, with a picture of a snowdrift, captioned: *We all know what happened that year.*

Yes and no. Fewer people talk about the connection between Love Canal and the Blizzard of 1977, even though both crises pushed the federal government to form agencies for managing disasters. Buffalo's pleas for help with snow removal helped to create the Federal Emergency Management Agency. And Love Canal spurred the creation of a war chest for cleaning up disasters, opening the way for Congress to pass the Superfund, whose official name is CERCLA, the Comprehensive Environmental Response, Compensation, and Liability Act. Superfund established the model of taxing industry to fund cleanup, the model of "polluter pays."

But beyond these political connections, there was another link between the blizzard and the canal. Over the spring and summer of 1977, all that snow and ice thawed, dwindling as it does until only small glaciers remained in the corners of parking lots and in the deepest shades of the north-facing woods. All across Niagara County, the groundwater rose with the rush of new melt. And the chemicals at Love's abandoned waterway rested a little less easy.

Many people know the stories about the dump that began to make their way into the press. People complained of places where dogs burned their noses just from sniffing. One woman kept returning her twins' sneakers because she thought their soles were defective. Then she realized the chemicals in her basement were eating away the rubber. Down the street, Lois Gibbs read the articles in the paper and began to wonder about her son, who had developed epilepsy after starting kindergarten at the school on the canal. Agnes Jones and Elene Thornton, renters who lived in the Griffon Manor housing project, began to organize their neighbors, too. Thornton had lost her two-year-old son to leukemia, and she had questions about why he had been sick. People who lived in Love Canal observed how their yards were defoliating. They got headaches after fixing their sump pumps or spending time in their basements. At Griffon Manor, where the majority of tenants were Black, there were records of "severe sewer defects" and plumbing that gave off intense chemical smells.

Once people suspected that their own homes were contaminated, they had more trouble shrugging off their symptoms. Some worked in the factories and experienced (often lax) safety mechanisms at their jobs. They knew that these companies could be fallible when something leaked. As one resident said at a meeting, "When you can hear that whistle blow, it's too late."

Whether they realized it or not, Hooker had picked an unlikely place to keep their excesses hidden. Closest to the surface, the soil of the old canal site is made up of silt and sand. Below that, there's a thick layer of dense, soft clay that water can't easily saturate. As one health commissioner wrote in his report, "The clay strata acts as a barrier and creates a perched groundwater condition"—a polite way of saying that the area was a bathtub where contaminated water could move horizontally through the neighborhood more easily than it could move vertically into the earth. A place where snow could melt into the most lethal of waking dreams.

The chemicals went into the storm sewers. People could smell them as they passed each manhole cover and drain. They went into Black Creek, where they sometimes left visible residues. The chemicals went into the Niagara River, too. This was the 1970s—when people were just beginning to emerge from the era of dispersal as a recommended practice—from *the solution to pollution is dilution.*

The first thing I loved about Buffalo was its waterfront. How you could walk right up to the edge of Lake Erie on crumbling piers covered with grass and Queen Anne's lace, how the deer made trails through the unmanicured lushness of meadows nobody had mowed. As Matt walked next to me through the grasses, I could feel him watching me take in the shoreline, the skyway, the wind-mills turning above a beach where there was once heavy industry. Chimney swifts nested in the smokestacks of abandoned factories, circling through evenings when the sun was an eyelid of fire lower-ing itself in the haze. Matt's job had brought us here, but I was the one who would ultimately need this place to hold us, to become our more-than-temporary home. The day Matt and I unpacked our first boxes was the longest day of the year. In the suspended time of a late northern solstice, we wandered down to the water and saw that there was a point where the path turned into a jetty, where you could walk out between the lake and the river, balancing for at least a mile on the shift between shades of blue.

One afternoon, I met an artist from our neighborhood named Chantal Calato, who grew up across the Little River from Love Canal. When I asked her about it, she told me that when she was in grade school, she and her classmates would ride the school bus down one of the abandoned streets. Among the weeds and trash, the driver would brake and swing his red stop sign into the absence of traffic. And the yellow door would open to pick up a boy.

Every day they drove up to his house, but the boy kept to himself. Chantal lived only a mile away, but she knew there was something different about his neighborhood. She could see the chain-link fences and overgrown grass from the front door of her mother's house on Cayuga Island—and she and her best friend sometimes peered across the wisp of the Niagara River that separated their homes from Love Canal.

The boy on her bus would slide into his seat without talking. Though she tries, Chantal can't remember his name. "He was an outcast," she says. "He was living in an outcast world."

～

In 1978, the testing and discovery of compounds like benzene, toluene, and dioxin at Love Canal shifted the psychogeography of the neighborhood. No one knew how far the chemicals from the dump had spread. In the press, "Love Canal" became shorthand for the whole area, not just the dump itself. Streets that had once been part of the larger grid of Niagara Falls became emptying rings around the bulls-eye of the hole. Ring I meant the houses adjacent to the dump, the first to be vacated and bought by the government. Ring II included the houses across the street. Instead of an extending patchwork of city blocks, the neighborhood became concentric, orbiting the origin of its suffering.

The people who lived beyond Ring II were not convinced it was safe. Some residents of Griffon Manor had lived in the neighborhood longer than the homeowners, and remembered the fires and explosions in the dump before it was covered over. They had health problems and couldn't *just* pick up and move.

When the health department was slow to answer their questions, some of the women in the neighborhood decided to undertake their own data collection. Overseen by Beverly Paigen, a researcher and biologist at Roswell Park cancer center, they became a small army of community scientists, surveying the area by phone and on foot, collecting lists of their neighbors' diagnoses, and relaying them back to Paigen to analyze. When Gibbs overlaid their findings on a map of the neighborhood, she saw that health problems were clustered in the wetter areas. Paigen also became convinced that the chemicals were moving through the groundwater, and presented this idea to the state health department in Albany. But they dismissed the research as "housewife data."

When local officials realized the problem was too big and expensive to solve at the state level, it created a conflict of interest. The crisis erupting at Love Canal threatened to shine a spotlight on the 609 other hazardous-waste sites discovered in New York State, not to mention the federal government's role in the development of chemical weapons in the area. Overwhelmed by the scale of the problem, several politicians who were originally supportive started trying to discredit the women. Western New York is still divided over the issue. Some people want stories like Love Canal to go away, to insist that it's all in the past. Some remember grandparents who took patriotic pride in their wartime work, even as it exposed them to hazardous waste. Others insist that the future depends on people who remember these disasters, on the community scientists and activists who learned how to hold officials and executives responsible.

Many have tried to give the Love Canal story an ending, to contain the narrative within a given moment in time. The story most people tell concludes in the fall of 1980, when lame-duck President Carter signed the Superfund into law. Anyone within the boundaries of the neighborhood who wanted to leave would be bought out of their mortgages or given moving assistance. But in practice, the trauma of living in uncertainty didn't resolve so fast. The homeowners who stayed watched their neighbors pack vans and trucks, tying furniture to the tops of cars. They found themselves pruning the shrubs in gardens their neighbors had fled, or walking down sidewalks past boarded-up houses. Even after a successful activist campaign for moving assistance, many renters faced discrimination and had to wait longer for new low-income housing placements. The longer they stayed in Love Canal, the more they were asked to tolerate, and the lonelier their surroundings became.

Hooker's executives hoped the bad publicity was over. The story was remediated. Contained. Safe. The chemicals are still in the ground. But it's safe. As Anne Boyer argues, *fuck cancer* has always been the wrong slogan when the cells of our bodies rebel. In a place where known hazards are buried, it would be better to say "Fuck white supremacist capitalist patriarchy's ruinous carcinogenosphere."

Before Buffalo, I'd never heard the phrase "environmental liens." I was at an art department gathering, standing around with Matt's new colleagues in a grain silo that had been turned into an event space. Onstage, an artist with bedazzled lips shimmied in front of a screen playing clips of a "We Buy Houses" seminar. As darkness fell in the concrete chamber, we could see only rhinestones, crusting a wolfish smile. At the bar, people were advising Matt on the problems of trying to find a raw space for a studio. Lead paint, leaking roofs. *You know, some of these old gas stations and industrial buildings, you have to make sure they don't have a tank buried, that they don't have any environmental liens.* It was real estate language for the cost of finding unfinished toxic cleanups—but said so casually that I caught myself nodding. As if it were common sense to think of pollution as an unpaid debt, a creditor about to repossess the house.

Among our neighbors on the West Side of Buffalo, some questions were less than casual. Did we like to garden? Grow vegetables? If so, we needed raised beds. Did we like to swim? If so, we shouldn't get in the water too close to the city. But each summer brought softer days, when the lake and the sky were twin mirrors of upside-down blue. An ailanthus tree came into leaf outside our window, growing from the churned dirt where the foundations of our house had been dug. People told us it was a junk tree, that we should cut it, but I watched birds in the branches instead—vireos, goldfinches, the bright crowns of kinglets. Before long we gravitated toward a patch of woods by the Buffalo harbor where wrens made nests in the reeds. Here, healing over the landscape didn't mean forgetting—placards informed us that this, too, had been a dump site, but its second life had the promise of a place where wildlife had started to return. Rippled with muskrats and gulls, the lagoon had a ruderal feeling: the sense of an ecosystem thriving among ruins, thriving all the more furiously because it had once been bare. I was beginning to know these places in all their damaged, green chaos, to love them with a kind of abandon.

Through pure coincidence, the streets in our neighborhood are named for the states we've left behind. Massachusetts, Rhode Island. I often turn onto Connecticut Street, past the bookstore whose window holds titles on harvesting honey, combatting soil pollution, cultivating medicinal plants. One evening I wandered down to meet Luella Kenny, one of the few early Love Canal activists who still lives in the area. At the height of the crisis, she'd kept a log of chemical disturbances in her backyard, and I asked her about it as the bookstore filled with people from our neighborhood who were waiting to hear her story.

I showed up at the bookstore that night because I'd sensed that disaster itself is only the beginning. That to live near a community dispersed by pollution is to consider how loss travels, and how memory travels. To wonder who watches the remnants of toxicity, and who makes sure that what's buried isn't forgotten.

When Luella Kenny moved to Love Canal before the crisis, she had a redbrick house and two boys who played in the stream. Eventually, she and her husband had a third son. Her property line was Black Creek itself—the last house before the shallow waterway merged with another creek that feeds the Niagara River. As she puts it, her family lived at the "confluence" of all these waterways. She and her husband earned modest salaries from their work in public health, and they'd chosen the house in part for the backyard—far bigger than your average city lot.

Then, in 1978, her youngest son, Jon Allen's, body suddenly swelled, and he was diagnosed with allergies. And then with nephrosis. Many of his symptoms were idiopathic, meaning his doctors could not locate their origins. He would be hospitalized, improve, and then return home and sicken. Though his doctors expected him to recover, Jon Allen's body revolted. Just two weeks after his seventh birthday, he died.

In the wake of Jon Allen's death, a consultant and a toxicologist for the state came to sample the water in the creek behind Luella's home. Stephen Lester, the consultant, detailed the sampling visit in his daily reports, where he noted that a bird had collapsed and died after drinking from the creek near the storm sewer outfall. Then, as Luella tells it, the toxicologist collecting samples looked at her as if she'd planted the bird to keel over on cue, as if she'd staged the moment for his benefit. Luella's face turns rueful, and she laughs. "I mean, I wish I had such mystical power. I would've used it a long time ago."

Later, the state informed her that the bird had died of a virus. How alienating, how strange, to be told what these people were told. "*It's fine,*" Luella parodies, "*it's safe. But don't you dare go in your basement. Don't you dare plant a garden, or if you do don't eat the fruits of that garden. But it's safe.*" Neat lines of demarcation were impossible to draw—how do you tell one sick person to evacuate, and tell another sick person across the street that they are outside the boundary of danger? The Love Canal activists had the painful task of advocating for the dispersal of their own neighborhood communities, for separation from their very own homes.

Though she hadn't initially suspected it, Luella began to look for answers about her son's death in the landscape—in that familiar double lot bordered by a creek, in the ideal neighborhood that had become uninhabitable. As objectively as she could, she began recording what she saw in the backyard, because she thought the state might want her notes for their investigation. Strange coatings appeared by the water, crystals of orange precipitate. "8/20/79, 8:30 a.m.," Kenny's log of the outfall reads,

> Water is semi-clear, level is ¼ way up drain. Orange is present on both sides of drain with deep orange almost brown globules on surface. . . . Oil is visible on the surface of Black Creek just before the vegetation.

> 8/20/79, 3:00 p.m. Water clear, level is at bottom lip of drain. Orange color present on both sides of drain. Some oil slicks present in channel from drain and around into main creek. Heavy Love Canal odor permeating entire yard since noon. Orange is present on bed of creek near where Bergholtz Creek is met. Heavy black tar-like material on our bank.

> 8/21/79, 7:30 a.m. Water semi-clear, level is just above bottom lip of drain. Orange color present on left side of drain. Oil present on surface all the way down the creek to junction of Bergholtz and Cayuga. . . . Odor (Love Canal) is present when you reach creek.

Eventually she writes, "The odor entered the house."

~

When it finally arrived in 1980, the money to relocate families away from Hooker's dump was funneled through the newly created Love Canal Area Revitalization Agency, or LCARA, a name that twists in the mouth. At first, I searched to see if there had been an intermediate name for the aftermath—but no, "revitalization" was already the word in 1980, even as the mass exodus isolated the neighborhood and scattered its communities. Michael O'Laughlin, chairman of the agency's board and mayor of Niagara Falls, made sure that getting the people out was coupled with redeveloping Love Canal, smoothing over the scar, getting new people back in.

Right away, the board slammed into the question of "habitability," which comes up again and again in the minutes of their meetings— a strange word, hemmed in by the performative language of *Robert's Rules of Order*. For Mayor O'Laughlin, habitability was a bogeyman that kept interfering with his resolutions to resettle the area. Who would determine such a quality? The Environmental Protection Agency, the attorney general, the health department? No one, to the mayor's knowledge, had ever needed to declare a piece of land habitable before. And if the land was indeed uninhabitable, shouldn't someone order the remaining Love Canal families to leave? LCARA's mission was to repair and repopulate the neighborhood. No one ordered the families to leave.

Ultimately, the EPA took on the task of performing a habitability study. To Mayor O'Laughlin's great dismay, a final decision about the land wouldn't arrive for nearly a decade. In the meantime, LCARA was stuck presiding over four hundred overgrown lawns, a fleet of decaying homes, and a half-empty housing project.

Despite security guards employed by LCARA, the area resisted improving. In the night, people came and lit fires. They stripped the copper wires from the remaining structures and dumped their old mattresses and trash. By the late eighties, the agency was renting out some of the properties, but they were concerned about the perception that they were slumlords. A whole page of meeting minutes is devoted to finding the cheapest bulbs they could use to keep the porch lights on every night in the abandoned houses.

By 1988, the EPA study was complete, and the health commissioner ruled that the land north of the canal (where Kenny had lived) and the land west of the canal (where Griffon Manor stood) were remediated and safe for unrestricted use. But the land to the east of the canal was uninhabitable. In the end, the fear lay too heavy on the streets of homes bordering the first evacuation rings. They were torn down and the materials were collapsed into the basements, the foundations backfilled and planted with grass.

North of Colvin Boulevard, though, Mayor O'Laughlin got his way. The houses were evaluated and the assessor assured the agency that "to have any market value at all, the appraisers must make the assumption that the subject sites are not contaminated with hazardous wastes and . . . that the properties are free from any potential environmental liens." As soon as the area was declared habitable, LCARA pivoted, becoming a full-blown real estate company with a sales office and a packet of disclosures they gave to each new resident.

The forces that drew people to Love Canal were the same forces that had populated the area in the first place. Nice backyards, space for gardens. The longing to own a home, to build a modicum of security. The houses were cheap. They were starter homes for young families. They were in a neighborhood that had a baseball diamond. Some people were willing to risk it, to live next to a gash in the landscape. To the revitalization agency, disclosure was enough for ethical absolution. But when the forces that draw people to a place are economic, the risks aren't simply voluntary. By poisoning the land, Hooker inadvertently created a place where the lure of a cheap house required people to wager on an imprecise knowledge of their "tolerance" for pollution. Mayor O'Laughlin at last got to enact the plan he'd been cultivating since 1982, when he'd told LCARA they should "use the subjective approach. It seems to me," he said, "we must move along in the best conscience and let people buy a house and move in at the appropriate time and listen for the echo."

I discovered Chantal Calato's work when I was looking for aerial photos of Love Canal and Model City. On her website, she has a series of images that plot how her personal geography entangles with the history of the land William Love deserted. Her parents are divorced, and as a child in the eighties, she would leave the island just outside Love Canal where her mom lives to spend time with her dad at his house in the woods near Model City, which is now a patchwork of hazardous-waste management companies, including one that's owned by the federal government and still houses waste and residues from nuclear projects and uranium processing. The site is now 191 acres with an ominous, understated name: NFSS, the Niagara Falls Storage Site. Chantal's father bought his property without knowing about the dump, and she and her brothers played in the trees out back. She was in her late twenties before she learned about the radioactive material left over from the Manhattan Project. "The danger, camouflaged by lush woods," she writes, "is surrounded by a porous chain-link fence."

Then there's Chantal's brother Joe, who lives just outside the boundary of Love Canal—one block from where the original families were bought out by the government. At forty-one, he was diagnosed with multiple myeloma, a rare cancer for someone so young. Joe is a drummer who spent hours practicing down in his basement. On a street of well-maintained suburban bungalows, his house sometimes flies a skull and crossbones flag. At one point, he put a sign out front with a slogan from one of the original Love Canal protests: *I've got better things to do than sit around and be contaminated!*

Chantal tells me that curious people sometimes stop her when they're driving around the suburban edge of Niagara Falls, looking for Love Canal. *Where is it?* they say. *I don't see it.*

⌒

The owners of Love Canal became Hooker Chemical became Occidental Chemical became Glenn Springs Holdings Inc. Love's legacy, and Hooker's, are nearly invisible to those who don't know about the ways the military-industrial complex is still buried and circulating through the soil. But it exists in the conduits of groundwater, in the uncertainty of those who are ill and don't know why, and those who can't afford to leave. What happened between the canal and Model City raises questions about who gets to ask for trust and whose trust is extracted and broken. Who has the privilege of information—and who has the privilege of flight. The traces contained in the earth and those that move through a person, all the invisible ways someone hosts the daily sites where they've eaten and swum and slept, the incremental buildup of toxins that is sometimes called the body burden.

There are so many stories, known and unknown, each a person who cast their shadow on this landscape and carried it with them when they fled. The dispersal of chemicals into the environment ultimately risked the dispersal of communities, too. "We are not above the laws of ecological reciprocity," writes Lisa Wells in her book *Believers: Making a Life at the End of the World*. When people poison the landscape, it starts to poison us back. The trouble at Love Canal, and at many other hazardous sites, was that the people who had the most to gain from dumping chemicals into the ground were not the same people at risk of exposure. I think of Hooker now when I see the signifiers of toxicity: chain-link clearings in the woods, chain-link around slopes of dandelions, chain-link running along both sides of a creek.

That first summer in Buffalo, our next-door neighbor worked in her garden while her six-year-old showed me the trees they climbed barefoot, the edges of the yard where the dog hid bones, the beds that yielded a fistful of weedy wild red strawberries. As soon as we moved in, they drew a picture of Matt and me, our names tangled together inside a heart, with flowers they'd picked stuck through the paper. We put it on our mantle—the first piece of art in our new home.

As we got to know each other better, my neighbor warned us about why part of our yard might have been paved—about lead and other heavy metals in the soil. I tried to reconcile what she'd said with the conversations around her firepit, where we met housing advocates and urban farmers, the roses and wisteria twisting around her doors, the stump in her yard as big as a table—what remained of the ash tree that fell after her father died, the tree whose logs heated her house through winter after winter, whose rings numbered the years he'd been alive. All the ways we tie ourselves to a place and its meanings.

When I stopped commuting, we also planted a garden with the help of our neighbors—jackhammering concrete, digging weeds, and filling wheelbarrows with dirt. Though we rototilled the ground to make a flower bed, a forest of surprise tulips still returned. How we were lucky like that, over and over, how the city did speak to us of its secrets, of its particular grammars of home.

It took Chantal months to tell her brother she was making art about his house. She drew plans, built rooms for a scaled-down model of his mail-order bungalow—the kind of house you can walk around in and get a sense of déjà vu. Chantal liked that familiarity. It made her think that others could look at this house and recognize their own spaces. When she finally worked up the courage to ask if she could interview him for her project, it was anticlimactic. *Sure, okay*, he told her. He would be part of her work.

That afternoon, I'd come to visit Chantal at her studio, where an arched window let in light through the old industrial glass. A cluster of jade plants sat prettily on a stand—a green interruption in the panes.

I'd come to talk to her about an installation she'd made called *Unseen*, which used a model of her brother's white house as the centerpiece. Except it wasn't white anymore—Chantal had remade the bungalow entirely out of dirt. In the middle of an unlit black box gallery, the porch light shines out of the gloom, illuminating the fuzzy darkness of a tall dirt pedestal, as if the earth beneath the house had been plucked out by a precise and remediating god. At the base of the pedestal, the deepest geological strata, an eerie purple light oozes out—the half-life of what's still buried. When people come to see *Unseen*, they circle the house like underground currents of water, looking at it almost from a dirt's-eye view. Though she didn't tell people exactly whose house it was, she did include a couple of identifying details. Through the back door, you can see steps down into a basement with a tiny drum kit. And the porch light always stays on.

Around the fulcrum of the model home, Chantal filled the air with voices—from hours of interviews with eighteen people whose lives have been altered by living next to contaminated sites in the area. In the darkened room, you can hear the tones shifting and blending in clusters, certain conversations gathered in each corner of the room as you move through the space. Over nine months of work, through her own health scares and those in her family, Calato kept listening. She showed me the charts she made as she thought through the audio, the painful categories necessary to create this chorus of voices. *Cancer/skin/other*, one reads. *Playing outside/snow melting/rain.*

"There's no bugs at Love Canal," one voice says. Another voice mentions that the deer near Model City had strange growths and the hunters wouldn't eat them; how there's the hesitation that comes from knowing there is radioactivity nearby. Humans habituating to the strangeness, but never knowing if, down the road, there would be a cost. One voice calls his childhood in the creeks of Model City a "lottery" you didn't want to win. "When I grew up there," says another, "we kind of got used to it and accepted it as normal. It's weird how people can adjust to things." "It's your normal to have those smells . . . ," says a third, "and if you're not talking to other people, you just kind of think, Oh, it's just our house."

As I listened, I realized *Unseen* knits a fabric that had come unraveled—layering scattered, individual experiences into a salvaged community whose stories resonate with one another. As somebody falls into silence, another picks up the thread, adding to the archive of absences that have become normalized. Even though some people have since left the area, their questions circle the places where their own lives have touched this landscape. Who are these places habitable for? When does the idea of home cause too much hurt? I wanted to ask Chantal why people stayed at Love Canal, and why they resettled the area even after it was abandoned. But this is in many ways an outsider's question. As if the answer isn't individual to every person who weighs the potential toxicity of the land against every other piece of their situation. When I ask Chantal why she thinks people come back to Western New York, she just nods and says "for family."

Chantal's interview with her brother is part of *Unseen*, too. In the darkness, you can pick out his voice, gentle, with a hint of weariness. He's talking about his first hematologist appointment, when his diagnosis was still brand-new. The doctor asked if he was from Niagara Falls. Then he asked if Joe lived near Love Canal. "Then," Joe says, "I followed up with the why. Is that, you know, why I have this cancer? Is this what caused this? It just struck me that he would ask me if I lived in Love Canal." Joe takes a breath. "He must have had something . . . in his mind."

It's safe to say that O'Laughlin's echoes still return, but only for those who are willing to hear them. Kenny tells me that every day, someone calls from her old neighborhood, sick or seeking advice. The waterway behind her old house was ultimately dredged three times to remove contaminants. The storm sewers were sealed. Then the Love Canal neighborhood was rebranded "Black Creek Village" after the stream where Jon Allen played and fished.

As I sit with her in her kitchen, Luella spreads a small sheaf of pictures on the tablecloth, pictures of her house in the eighties, when it was owned by the Revitalization Agency after her family fled. In the photos, her vandalized garage doors sag, and plaster trails from the ceiling. Walls gape where the wires have all been stripped. Each time I pick up a photo, I touch the delicate print of Luella's tablecloth—pale gray checkerboard, flecked with yellow flowers and cherries.

Among the community leaders, Luella's old house at Love Canal is the only one that still stands. These days, if you google her former address, you'll find a real estate listing. The exterior brick has been painted HGTV gray. The interior has been redone with a nautical theme—ship's wheels, starfish, points of the compass rose. "Move-in ready all brick ranch with stunning curb appeal on Cayuga Creek!" reads the sales pitch. "'Park-like' double lot that features 2nd garage/shed with electric, firepit, gazebo." The listing even dares to advertise the "water access," though the creek is fenced. Nonetheless, she tells me that three different families have lived there. One woman even held her daughter's wedding in the yard. I wondered if there were photos from that day, and if the dredged creek might shimmer in the background, an unnamed and unwelcome guest.

Sometimes the closer you are, the less you want to know. Even with proximity, even on the scale of a neighborhood, it's hard to share the loss that comes with separating yourself from a damaged place. The owners of the Love Canal site work with the EPA to maintain the pumps and filtration systems around the dump "in perpetuity," but the chemicals are still in the ground to this day. One person in the audience asked if Luella could say anything about the role of historical amnesia—how much can hide in a name, how much a name can remember. "The people that moved in, they don't want to hear it called Love Canal . . . ," she said. "Fortunately, the name still sticks."

One afternoon, I ask Chantal if people ever talked about the Manhattan Project when she was growing up in the area. She tells me she never heard about it. Like most people, I'd been quick to think about atomic history in Oak Ridge and Los Alamos, not in Western New York. But the Manhattan Engineer District had a field office in the area, and several factories along the Niagara River were crucial to the secret development of the bomb the US dropped on Hiroshima. Hooker Chemical handled uranium ores and made products for the refining process. Steel plants just outside Buffalo figured out how to work with the metal. Just six miles away from where we live, a company named Linde Air Products was deeply entangled in refining ores and enriching uranium for nuclear fuel. As government documents reveal, Linde created one of its worst messes in the 1940s with the explicit knowledge of the army, which allowed the company to dump radioactive sludge into wells on the plant's property. When you combine these sites, Love Canal appears as one highly publicized part in a larger story of how the US government weaponized the companies along the Niagara River, and how civilians live alongside the waste created by wartime manufacturing.

Love's Model City is now partly managed by the US military under a program called the Formerly Utilized Sites Remedial Action Program, which was created for remediating places that were contaminated by early atomic projects. The "cleanup and consolidation" of radioactive material didn't begin at the site until the 1980s, when, in the wake of Love Canal, a scathing report for the New York State Assembly Task Force on Toxic Substances detailed the army practice, at Model City, of "dumping radioactive wastes in open and often unmapped pits, in rusting barrels stacked along the road side, and in inadequate structures originally designed for different purposes." Eyewitnesses remember army trucks dumping drums at Love Canal, too, but the military still denies it.

Much was shrouded in "buffer" land, and in secrecy. Though the NFSS parcel at Model City haphazardly became one of the earliest radioactive waste dumps in the US, the remediation in the eighties was intended to be a temporary solution. An "Interim Waste Containment Structure" was built to house the half-life of the Arsenal of Democracy. The ultimate decision was to move the waste offsite, but as I write, that hasn't happened yet. Model City is about twenty-five miles from Buffalo. But many people don't know that these traces are still there.

At the doctor's office for a checkup, I notice the nurse's questions now include a screening for loneliness. As I sit on the thin paper, she asks if I live by myself or if I'm married and how many times in the last week I've talked to my family or friends. I don't tell her that after two years and two months, I note each stem of chicory flaunting blue pinwheels at the edge of our street, or that because they seeded themselves, these plants are called volunteers. I don't tell her that by now, I've lived in our house in Buffalo longer than any other home since I turned eighteen.

One evening, Matt and I walk to a park in our neighborhood to meet up with some friends, including two who are expecting a baby. It's a warm night in June. Matt and I bring a picnic blanket to spread in the grass by the Niagara River, and as we sit, he brushes a leaf from the part of my hair and presses his shoulder against mine.

I'm still a little in awe of these gifts of duration—to see friends after work on the spur of the moment, to sip at will from the pool of shared days until you begin to feel like family. We listen to them talking under the trees on the riverbank, about mothers and new parenthood and how it feels to realize they'll be settled here for a while once the baby arrives.

Sprawled in the grass, one of us looks up to notice that the tree above us is a cherry, that the branches are full of fruit. And before I know what to say, one of our friends is up in the branches, laughing and spilling cherries down by the handful as the sun sets and the river casts gold filaments of deep, fast current. And Matt is looking at me expectantly while I think about how this park is also a dump capped over, how I know this is a mature tree whose roots go deep into the groundwater, how there's a sign by the path with red Xs over the kinds of fish people catch here and recommendations about how often it's advisable to eat them (for pregnant women: never). How the same river that moves through the gills of the fish is moving below us, in the riverbank that feeds the tree.

And I don't want to speak up, but I have to, because maybe they don't know. And I watch as the softness of the evening fractures and my friends start asking me questions I can't answer, like is it okay to eat just a few? They want to believe the luck of abundance, all these fat cherries just waiting on the banks of the river. And my face flushes hot with shame because these are people I love, and even saying *I don't know if it's safe to eat them* is to break something that feels irreparable. I've put a wedge between us and the place we want to settle into, and that isn't what I hoped learning this land-scape would do.

The writer Daisy Hildyard argues that contemporary lives have a division between a first and a second body—that everyone has a body that moves through the world doing ordinary tasks, traveling to and from work and spending time with our families. But each of us also has a second body, the part of us that's entangled with melting ice, and pollution, and the carbon footprint of takeout orders. Under the tree, I think about the dissonance of toxicity, how you often can't see it or feel it or taste it—how we each have a body that wants to see a cherry as a cherry, as a discrete, contained thing, and how we also have a body that encounters that cherry as the fruit of the soil and its history, something that has its own second life through the chemicals it carries and their potential effect on our cells. But I think, too, that maybe I am overreacting—that no one can say, without testing, whether it's unsafe to eat these cherries. The question is really about risk, transparency.

Yet when it comes to other living beings, the ethics of these disclosures no longer apply. No one can tell a bird that a plaque advises them not to eat the fish, or that there has been discussion of the acceptable number of parts per billion. As sites of pollution grow weeds and grasses and trees, as they're turned into parks or scars or containment areas, the line between voluntary and involuntary risk grows fuzzy. When the land no longer looks like a dump, it's easy to return to a kind of innocence about what happened here. But without learning the devastated history of these places, I also wouldn't understand why their abundance is such a complex, fragile victory. I wouldn't understand that there is also an ecological reciprocity to remediation—when people are able to clean up these sites properly, they become more and more hospitable. They have an enormous capacity to heal.

On a Tuesday in May, nearly a year to the date after my first visit to Love Canal, Chantal and I walk in South Buffalo at one of the parks near the water. When we get out of the car, we watch a snake swim through a man-made pond, its tail carving a ridge into the surface of its wake. This is Tifft Nature Preserve, a place where wild deer and birds shelter in deep thickets of honeysuckle and native cattails,

where trails loop through marshes, and crows make winter rooker-
ies on islands of abandoned grain elevators. Where green alleys of
brush give way to shivering drifts of apple blossom. Some trees are
old, voluminous. Left over from when the land was a farm.

Chantal and I climb the Mounds, a group of low hills behind the
parking lot. As we gaze over the brightness of the water, Chantal
asks why this place is called a nature preserve when the ground we
stand on is actually landfill, a quadrant of bulges where the worst of
the pollution from the site is gathered and capped. The fly ash, slag,
and abandoned drums are invisible now, but Chantal is right—like
the Fens, this place isn't "preserved nature"—it's a massive remediation project.

I wanted to walk here in part because I'd been struggling. Sometimes
it feels wrong, disrespectful, even, to be drawn to the sites of these
cleanups—like a kind of morbid fascination. That same week, I'd
caught up with a friend who lives in another city, and she'd asked
me if researching the history of the area had made me want to move.
My palm sweating into the phone, startled by the question, though
of course I could follow her logic. How could it be that learning the
land was contaminated doesn't make me love it any less? How could
I explain that when these acres lose their use value to industry or
real estate, they're both discarded and, in a strange sense, set free?
These places unauthorized for normal human use are still home to
bacteria or microorganisms or seedlings of weeds. They still begin,
as my friend Jen put it, to render themselves outside a system we
fully understand. Maybe it's as simple and inescapable as this: when
we chose this place to live—when, in a time of ecological loss, we
were lucky enough to choose—we also chose the aftermaths and
possible futures grounded here.

As Chantal and I leave the Mounds and walk into the heart of the
park, we emerge from shade trees into a wetland's flooded edge.
Chantal tells me she sometimes looks at this forest and wonders what

it will be like in fifty years, when her young kids are grown up. At least four species of swallows dive around us, eating bugs at the edge of the water. When we turn back to look at the woods, a small forest of tubes protects native seedlings from beavers and deer—an effort to restore the full variety of species that once grew here. And I realize that watching this transformation is another great privilege of staying.

On the way back to our neighborhood, Chantal tells me that many people react to *Unseen* as if it's just about Love Canal, and just about Love Canal forty years ago. But her installation holds space for a whisper network that is still unfolding all across the area. Each voice is a testament to the long history of polluted places, and each needs to be listened to—because if there's anything definitive to know about these landscapes, it's that stories of toxicity may have echoes, but they don't have endings.

It doesn't help the future life of these damaged landscapes to ignore those who are most sensitive to contaminants. The voices of chronic illness and toxicity are not separate, outlier experiences, but a fundamental piece of human reciprocity with landscape. And the Rust Belt is not alone—nearly a quarter of people in the US live within three miles of a Superfund site. *Unseen* is applicable to so many places where the ground conceals caches of waste that weren't mapped or recorded.

At Tifft, what will grow on the soil sometimes provides the best clue to what was buried there. Phragmites, stiltgrass, pine. A doe stopping in the path to look at us, the light glowing through the skin of her delicate ears. The discovery and removal of 116 chemical drums, some of which contained naphthalene.

As we turn toward the West Side, I ask Chantal about amnesia, about forgetting. "How do you lose a memory," she asks, "when it was never even really known?"

Just recently, a friend stood next to me outside after a reading. In the matter-of-fact tone of a local, he told me that as a child, he used to play at Love Canal, that the chemicals in the grass melted his shoes. I was too shy to ask if he worried about that exposure—too aware of the stigma that still haunts Cataract City, the former honeymoon capital, the empty storefronts of Niagara Falls. When you look at a tourist map of the city, the scale has been warped to elide all the land that made up its most infamous neighborhood. None of the streets that mark its boundaries are labeled. This was Mayor O'Laughlin's wish to forget, to revitalize—the green oblivion of grass growing on the clay.

But those who advocate for remembering Western New York's toxic history understand that to feel the hurt in a place is also a form of love. In Chantal's studio, there's a scrap of paper with a handwritten list of her goals. The last item reads: *Make positive impact on Niagara Falls*. There's so much work to be done—to regulate, to remediate. Though the Superfund established the concept of "polluter pays," these days many cleanups are stalled, and the resources to finish them haven't been replenished. Here, as in so many places, there is a deep need for transparent information about the water and the land—to restore accountability and trust, and to replace containment structures that were only ever meant to be temporary.

It's tragic to me that with the warning signs gone, people can move to the very edge of Love Canal or Model City without ever hearing the story. But maybe, with the right amount of anger and irony, Black Creek Village could also be a name that holds the whole history it was devised to erase. After all, they named the subdivision after the waterway that became a vector of poison—carrying the runoff through backyards and drains, into the river itself.

Later, I talk to that same friend about stories whose names have held alternate meanings. And I think about how the evolution of a landscape, or a landmark, doesn't have to mean forgetting. About how places accumulate meaning for those who read into them, like the words for monuments or wars or streets. I knew when we moved that nowhere is untouched by human interventions, but I didn't know we'd chosen a place that could hold such depths of loss and abundance and braid them together. That this, too, is a form of tending.

Each time I walked around Love Canal, I thought about Chantal's *Unseen* and the myriad invisible stories of illness that began in this place—that were, perhaps, still beginning. I repeated that word to myself as the wind kicked up a small current of dust, as it coated my lips and fingers, as I felt the temptation to wipe my mouth, as I remembered how *much unseen is also here.*

I still wouldn't trade the long afternoons I've spent in our backyard watching the light change color in the ailanthus tree, these accumulated days of wanting, and fearing, to be immersed. That even in scarred landscapes, a home can answer our longing—for closeness or company or regeneration. For muskrats and junk trees. For another chance at this dilapidated earth.

9

Shadow Count

Somewhere in those years of 6 a.m. flights, I developed a recurring dream of a place I knew in the northwesternmost corner of Connecticut, where stone walls snaked among the trees of a forest that had once been farmland. The kind of town where the post office is also home to two chipmunks, one messy and one clean. A place full of wild birds, the flocks of my earliest childhood, vortexes of robins where rural woods broke open into fields. Where I had dug in the streambed and drunk the shimmer of mica with the silt. Where old traces of human mining and clear-cutting had been softened by an enveloping abundance. I felt myself wanting to check on it, wondering how it was doing.

When I was a small child just learning to read, we lived for a time in the schoolhouse there, which overlooks a meadow. In the evening as the light fell, I would watch what I thought were swallows swooping over the tall grass, their movements jagged but graceful, mirroring the insects they chased. My father was the one who told me they were bats. We'd stand in the doorway as the wings disappeared into the darkness and the fireflies began their night signals, hovering over the field. I was learning to read the landscape, too—and with each word I became more connected, as the names of creatures unlocked the gates to concepts of dazzling strangeness. Bioluminescence. Echolocation. Ways of knowing that, as a kid, I held alongside my own senses, imagining what it would be like to have another means of perception.

But for too long I had allowed myself to hold what I remembered lightly, as if my father were a dictionary where I could always look up what I had forgotten. As the years passed without him, I could feel the specificity leeching from my language in the rare moments when I did try to talk about the living world. And how easy to let a term like "bird-watcher" stand in for who my father was, for the experience of walking with him at the lakeshore in the evening, for all the live movements and complications of a person. In the years since his death, I hadn't added new encounters, or new words, to the archive of experience we once shared. To keep the grief at bay, I held myself apart. And after a while, I felt I was losing him, letting him be consumed by the shorthand of memory. I could play back the tape—a man reaches down into the grass and squeezes a stem of toadflax. The flower opens and shuts like a mouth. The child, who had been whining, laughs.

Nostalgia can be a trap: the present eats the past as it loops on itself, until the act of reaching backward becomes more important than what's touched. Just when I think I've invented my father, I find a slide in a drawer and hold it up to the bright noon sky. I'm there in the frame, perhaps one year old, riding in a pack on his back, turning to stare at the camera. He is facing away, his gaze tipped up, scanning the trees with binoculars. The old stories are true—we were bird-watching before I could talk. But without trying to cultivate my own, present knowledge of a place, these stories alone don't satisfy me. I wear them away with time, and like statues, they become both polished and shabby.

"It is not possible," as the writer Barry Lopez puts it, "for human beings to outgrow loneliness." With time, as I got older and better at suppressing my feelings, my language for the world we'd shared became weaker and weaker, until I could no longer tell the difference between avoiding a memory and forgetting. When I paused to watch the flight of a bird I couldn't recognize, I was pinned by a namelessness that disturbed me, as if the creature itself were gone. In the end, I decided that if I could not outrun or outgrow longing, then the least I could do was notice it. Some things I'd shared with my father were lost, but I could still go to Cornwall, spend time in the schoolhouse, try to befriend the gaps in my knowledge, relearn what he had taught me. Better to live with the ache than not register what's missing at all.

One of the challenges biologists face is that it's very difficult to count an absence. Decades can pass between the last confirmed sighting of a species and the presumption that they are extinct. In the meantime, people search for any sign of their song, their markings, their tracks, exhausting the habitats that once sheltered them, trying to distinguish between what's rare and what's gone.

On my first morning in the woods, I opened a cabinet and found a pile of my father's bird books. One was a 1980 edition of Peterson's *Field Guide to the Birds East of the Rockies* with a cardinal on the faded cover. I let the book fall open where the spine had cracked and found a paragraph on the Bachman's warbler, which the guide called "the rarest North American songbird."

Even in 1980, though, the last sightings of Bachman's warblers were more than a decade old. When researchers in the late seventies conducted surveys looking for these birds, they played recordings of their calls to the landscape. At the time, other birds still responded to the sound of the endangered warblers with what the researchers described as "scolding"—as if they might still recognize the territorial nature of the Bachman's warbler from direct experience.

In 2002, researchers spent 166 hours going over Congaree National Park, where people had reported sightings in the past. A team of scientists and volunteers surveyed 3,900 acres, stopping every four hundred feet to search and to play recorded calls. But they didn't see or hear any Bachman's warblers. The researchers also noted that other birds had stopped responding to the calls—as if they no longer recognized their sound. By 2021, the US Fish and Wildlife Service proposed to "delist" this warbler, removing them from the endangered species category and concluding that these birds have, in all likelihood, become extinct. My father's guide had offered me a yellow-feathered ghost with a small black patch on its crown.

There's something eerie about a warbler whose habitat is a field guide, who exists only in drawings. But I like the way some bird books list even the most improbable sightings, offering a hope, if you can call it that, of a kind of resurgence. To leave out the nearly impossible would be anathema to the idea of species check-lists, of laying eyes or ears on as many birds as you can in a life-time. Though these birds are being delisted, the 2020 edition of the Peterson's guide still includes the Bachman's warbler. This stubbornness has a kind of beauty—a refusal to admit disappearance, to stop looking for what's hard to find.

But beyond extinction, there's another category that's easier to notice. Birds whose status is rated CBSD, for *common bird in steep decline*. This group of birds evokes Michael McCarthy's phrase "the great thinning"—the way familiar species have simply become less numerous, though they remain part of the landscape. A recent study in *Science* estimates that since 1970, the US has lost nearly three billion birds, an almost 30 percent decline in abundance. As populations of certain birds become smaller, questions emerge about when (and why) a decline reverses or accelerates.

Borrowing from the language of chemicals and pollutants, groups that estimate bird populations have used the concept of a half-life:

the number of years until there are half as many birds as there are today. For CBSDs, the estimates can be startlingly short. In 2016, Common grackles were given a half-life of just thirty-three years. If current trends continue, I'll be in my sixties when half as many grackles strut across grasses at dusk, shimmering like oil slicks in evening light. Chimney swifts, the "flying cigars" of the birder world, have a half-life of twenty-seven years. Blackpoll warblers have just sixteen. But these numbers are warnings, calls for greater action and attention—predictions that don't have to come true.

⌐

When numbers are diminishing, what someone counted in the past begins to gather special significance. Along with the field guides, I have a few of my father's bird lists. These are mainly from the years just before I was born, when my parents stayed in that one-room schoolhouse, where they added a tiny kitchen and a loft for sleeping. In these woods near the Housatonic River, my father spent hours watching birds. Sometime in the early eighties, he began participating in community science bird surveys with a group of volunteers who gathered data for scientists and conservation projects. He would wake up in the early hours and put on his skis or snowcats, combing through the winter woods for owls.

In these years before I was born, he participated in the Christmas Bird Count, the longest running community science bird survey in the US. The count began in 1900, after an ornithologist named Frank Chapman became concerned about sharp declines in several bird species. In New York City, where he worked at the American Museum of Natural History, he noticed that a lot of women were wearing whole birds or feathers on their hats, making the delicate white fronds of egret feathers into an overharvested commodity. And on Christmas Day, some people still organized "side hunts," where shooting parties would "hie them to the fields and woods on the cheerful mission of killing practically everything in fur or feathers that crossed their path."

As the editor of *Bird-Lore* magazine, Chapman argued that this behavior was unsportsmanlike. He proposed a different kind of "friendly" competition. Rather than killing the birds, he argued for a Christmas Bird Census, where groups of people would go out and see how many birds they could count on December 25. He offered to publish the results in his magazine. The first year, twenty-seven volunteers counted a total of ninety species. Over time, the parameters for counting solidified: each survey has to take place on a single day, and no birds can be included other than those seen during the twenty-four-hour period. (Though organizers are allowed to include a supplemental, separate category for species they see during "count week.") Each area is a fifteen-mile-wide circle, which can be divided into routes depending on the number of teams who participate in that area. Each circle also has a compiler, who gathers all the checklists and notes the "effort" and metadata—how many volunteers came out, for example, how long they worked, and the weather conditions. The team that sees the most species can consider themselves the best birders in the area.

Chapman fulfilled his purpose—the count has become robust enough that scientists continue to use the data gathered by those who participate. The results are now online, going back to 1900, and anyone can search them. Along with data from radar and other counts like the Breeding Bird Survey, which takes place in the spring, scientists and conservationists use the results of the Christmas Bird Count to estimate bird populations and measure which species are increasing or declining over time.

In my father's era, the count was quite competitive. In theory, anyone could join, but the compilers and route captains often relied on people they knew and trusted, to ensure that their circles produced accurate tallies. If you heard a snippet of a bird's call, you could count it—you didn't have to lay eyes on each one. Some people woke up in the early hours to go owling in the snowy woods, and stayed out to catch the dawn chorus. Organizers held potluck dinners late into the night, when the sightings from each route were checked and stats for each group were announced.

I suspect my father got involved with the bird count through his friend Mike Redmond, a seasoned naturalist who lives a little ways up the dirt road that winds past the schoolhouse. Mike's somewhat retired now, but in those days he was a logger, a caretaker of estates, a trucker who drove racehorses to Belmont and Saratoga. Once, he told me, he got stuck in a blizzard outside Rochester with a load of baby food and subsisted by slurping down a few jars in his cab. Despite sometimes being away for his job, his connection with the rural landscape goes deep, especially when it comes to birds.

When the two men found a great horned owl nest in the woods behind my father's driveway, it was Mike who set up the spotting scope so they could take a closer look without disturbing the birds. But beyond the easy friendship of two people in a tiny town who share a hobby, they liked going against the grain of each other's assumptions, or at least that's how it seemed to me. And my dad was amazed by the beauty of Mike's drawings. He could pencil the wing muscles of a red-tail without losing their power, and the eyes of his raptors delivered their mile-long stare. It is, I think, an intimacy with these creatures that allows him to draw them so well. He can really *see* how they maneuver; he's taken the time to hold their gaze.   .

Mike once got into trouble on a bird count because he crossed over into another birder's territory, looking for a Carolina wren. He was listening for the song—*teakettle-teakettle-teakettle*—when a woman started coming after him with her umbrella. In those days, the Christmas Bird Count in this area had around seventy participants, and together they often put in more than a hundred hours.

The numbers are smaller now, but in other areas they've grown. Mike still does the count each year. He says he'll be doing it when he's a hundred.

There's no substitute for his long knowledge of this place—including its human and nonhuman creatures. He remembers the way my dad took notes in the back of his bird book—a copy I've never been able to find. When I ran into Mike on the road near his home, more than twenty years had gone by since he'd last seen my father, but he wanted to tell me he'd been thinking about him. And in the scuff of dirt under my feet, I felt the viewpoint shifting, telescoping.

One morning, in the early hours of the 1986 Christmas Bird Count, my father had been out in the dawn woods, looking for owls with Mike. They'd gotten up at 5 a.m., trying to be quiet as their boots broke through the snow crust. They'd already heard two saw-whets and the urgent lilt of a great horned owl. After several hours, my dad could barely feel his toes, so he went home to warm up a bit and eat some breakfast before continuing the route. As he crossed out of the tree line, the schoolhouse door flew open and my mother came running out to meet him. She had just taken a pregnancy test. It seemed impossible, but after years of hoping and giving up, they were finally going to have a child.

When I began to look more carefully, I knew that some of the birds my father saw would be difficult for me to find. As many times as I walked these rural roads, I'd be hard-pressed to see an evening grosbeak or a purple martin—once-common species that are now rare here. Still, I knew from my translation work that if you want to learn from the dead, you have to visit their places. Just because a living landscape can never be a monument doesn't mean it can't hold the fleeting echo of a presence—the way an animal's shadow moves over grass blades on the ground. *I'm stepping on your head*, I used to say to him, as I followed him around the evening meadow, trampling through his silhouette. How the absence of light blooms for just a moment in that shadow—in mine, in my father's, in the wing shapes of every bird—before the grass returns to greenness.

Here the extraordinary feels possible, if elusive. That shadow in the trees could be a crow or the wings of a pileated woodpecker, emerging from a hole in the trunk. That knot in the tree could be a nest healed over. Those feathers, a bobcat's meal.

When I started relearning the birds, there was so much activity that sometimes it overwhelmed me. I could catch facets of what was happening, like looking through a kaleidoscope at a coral reef. I thought a lot in these early days about the visual grammar of bird-watching—wing bars, eye rings, streaks. Like learning any language, it was humbling. While I retained some foundations from walks with my father, I was rusty. I knew when something looked sparrowish in flight, and the way a flock of starlings shook loose from a tree with a rustle like dead leaves. I knew how red-winged blackbirds perched at the edges of the swamp like sentinels, displaying their bright epaulettes. But I'd forgotten some basic distinctions. How the flight of a goldfinch undulates, how they can seize on the head of a wildflower. How a phoebe's call is reedy, front-loaded, not sweet like a chickadee's. Many times I picked up the bird book thinking I'd seen something rare, only to realize what I'd been looking at was completely familiar. Perhaps out of a wish for anecdotal reassurance, I wanted to inhabit this place with the birds whose presence felt precarious before they swerved across my path. But my ear or eye had tricked itself. I'd been caught out by an assumption. I hadn't known enough context.

When I first spoke French outside a classroom, I'd experienced something similar—a testing of the signs I'd memorized against the living language as it actually moved through the world. Ça se dit pas, someone would say, to correct me. "That's not how you say it." But as a stranger in the language, I was shaken by the innate sense of violation in this phrase. *That's not how it says itself; that isn't how it communicates.*

Once, I looked up from my desk, startled at the number of birds I was hearing from a single thicket. In quick succession, I heard a robin, a blue jay, a red-winged blackbird. As the song continued, it was odd that the sounds didn't overlap—instead, they were rushed together, back-to-back, a chaotic tumble of familiar notes. This remix, I realized, was actually coming from a single gray catbird, a gorgeous mimic of other species whose cobbled-together song can last for ten whole minutes straight. That piling-on of sounds had a particular accent, which is how to tell a catbird apart from the species they copy.

Not long after, I encountered the reverse lesson. Up the road, I heard a blackbird, a blue jay, and the sharp *keeeer* of a red-tailed hawk. I thought a mimic might be singing. But no, when I got closer, all three species were perched together at the top of a tree. As I turned the corner, the hawk flew off, with the smaller birds hovering in pursuit. I was out of practice at noticing the habits of other species, but it was a relief to study creatures who can be known only in motion, in life, through experience and observation, resisting, at every moment, my attempt to contain them in static images or in words. Each morning, the birds left me off-balance—they turned me inside out.

❧

My father, too, had once found a way out of loneliness through birds. As a child, his school evacuated from London during the bombing raids of World War II. At age twelve, he suddenly became a boarder, safe but separated from his parents for months in a dank Bedfordshire country house someone had hastily offered as student housing. Homesickness wasn't patriotic. When my father moved on to a high school in Dorset, its reputation as "progressive" still included cold baths every morning. And a run before breakfast, which my father actually liked, until some classmates tripped him and he had to pick the gravel out of his knees.

He was happiest alone on long walks through the fields around the school, where he was more likely to meet a blackbird or a local farmer than one of his erstwhile peers. My father told me once that his only friend in those days was a lie—he'd conspired with another unpopular boy to pretend they were close on days when parents visited. His "friend" must have been equally miserable, though, because later that year, he tried to hang himself with his uniform tie.

At seventeen, in the middle of the war, my dad lost his own father. My grandfather had been working for the General Electric Company, racing to develop a radar apparatus that would be compact enough to fit on planes and accurate enough to detect the periscopes of German submarines. This job was high pressure, and his heart was bad. One day the headmaster of the boarding school summoned my father to his office to tell him the news. He heard secondhand that his mother had called from home, that his father was dead, and that she didn't recommend going to the funeral. There was no other explanation. My father didn't know what else to do but go back to the cafeteria, where he'd been drinking a cup of powdered hot chocolate. In the time it had taken to talk to the headmaster and return, the cocoa hadn't even gotten cold.

"As children, we know so little about our parents," he wrote to me before he died.

> We do not know the lives they led before we were born, and seldom see much of the work our fathers and mothers leave home each day to do. We define our parents by their parenting,

which means everything to us, but leaves so much out. I never even looked clearly into my father's face.

The boarding schools of wartime England were no place for grief. He didn't even tell his teachers or classmates that his father had died. Some found out, and sidled up to him so awkwardly that he ended up comforting them. But by that time he was old enough to have a less demanding school schedule. He could walk in the woods. He could make drawings from old natural history books. And he could watch birds in the field.

The biologist Robin Wall Kimmerer has written about what she calls "the grammar of animacy"—the ability to recognize, in language, the life-forces of the earth and of other species, "the wordless being of others in which we are never alone." She writes that in Potawatomi, the language of her ancestors, many things she had known in English as nouns were actually verbs. "To be a hill, to be a sandy beach, to be a Saturday, all are possible verbs in a world where everything is alive," she continues. "Water, land, and even a day, the language a mirror for seeing the animacy of the world, the life that pulses through all things, through pines and nuthatches and mushrooms." On the other hand, "A bay is a noun only if water is *dead*."

For those of us who are used to thinking in English, our language is wildly disadvantaged in this area. Many elements of the nonhuman world are referred to not just as nouns but as objects. English speakers don't usually extend the "who" to beings beyond the human. Sure, a pair of scissors is an "it," but so is a network of mycelium, homing through the soil in ways we're only beginning to understand. Why is a whip-poor-will an "it," when these birds say their names over and over in the dark, like metronomes on moonlit nights? When we know so little about their lives and perceptions, thanks, in part, to their perfect camouflage?

When you're lonely, it's hard to see yourself in the language of others. "The arrogance of English," Kimmerer writes, "is that the only way to be animate, to be worthy of respect and moral concern, is to be a human." As a result, exploitation can fester in the linguistic distance we make between ourselves and other species. For Kimmerer, "Saying 'it' makes a living land into 'natural resources.'" The alternative doesn't have to be anthropomorphism, though—that would be an equally arrogant co-option of other species. There is a space between objectification and assimilation that I might as well call respect. Respect might mean lying in bed listening to the call of the whip-poor-will through the skylight and wondering how the woods look to a nightjar, how she might perceive the shadows of branches and the shelter of leaf cover. It might look, as writers like Kimmerer and Ed Yong have recently argued, like finding the true expansiveness in our world through the understanding of nonhuman intelligences. The humility of knowing that as we live, other species are pursuing their own lives through worlds of their own perceptions—a vast cacophony of senses. A grammar of animacy where each verb is a different mode of existing.

The first time many birds migrate, they must do it innately, navigating to a place they've never been before. There's still a lot we don't know about this movement, but one theory is called the clock and compass, meaning that some birds are born with an instinct to move at certain times of the year and a direction they're driven to travel. Researchers have observed that when birds are in captivity, they will often experience nocturnal restlessness during seasons when they would normally be flying—rustling their wings at night as a manifestation of their instinct to move.

Beyond that first instinctive journey, birds use starlight, the earth's magnetic field, and other cues like local landmarks. There's evidence, too, that birds use the polarized light from the sunset to recalibrate their internal compasses on a daily basis. Some use the sun, too, if they're flying during daylight hours, but most birds migrate at night. The atmosphere is calmer and cooler then, and celestial markers are more visible, especially in places where their glow hasn't been dimmed by human-created brightness.

Mike told me that he sometimes goes up to Maine during fall migrations so he can watch birds through his scope as they cross the rising moon, identifying them by their silhouettes. When the seasons turned over, I, too, began studying at night, recording calls, out with my binoculars for long hours when I should have been writing, googling late into the morning until I could name everything I'd seen. I wanted to learn the language of field marks and identification, but I didn't want it to reduce or hollow out the mystery of these interactions with wild birds, these moments when my perception crossed their own.

I shouldn't have worried. Just by being alone in the woods, walking the paths, I'd already stepped into the thick of things. With each return visit to these woods and fields, patience and noticing come a little more easily. So do observations of other plants and animals. On a walk I note the severed front leg of a deer, its hoof crooked over the low branch of a pine. Bobcat mischief? Or the sign of a human hunt? Fresh death quickly ages, camouflages. Something will come for this hoof, and the last hint of its nourishment will vanish back into the mouth of the summer landscape. Until then, the leg in the tree is an invitation, a trace of decay on the air.

One evening, as I let the dogs out, I notice one of them step hesitantly toward the woods and bark low, a huff under his breath. I call and he comes closer, looking over his shoulder as he pees. Then he runs inside. It's the hour just before night, when things separate from their shadows and I retreat indoors, conscious of the acre of woods and fields between me and my nearest neighbor. From the doorway of the schoolhouse, I watch as a shape detaches from the black tangle of a toppled tree. At first, it looks like a man in a sweater, bent over, picking something up from the ground. I start to close the door and watch, heart in throat, as his face turns toward me. But it's a bear's face, a black bear, and the fear turns to something else entirely.

From my vantage, his movements are slow, deliberate, articulated—he's a young bear, tall, not too heavy. I see him moving between the trees, then lose him. The mullions are in my way. Ten minutes later, something shifts in the darkness, and he comes through the ferns, passing not ten feet from the window, moving like a condensation of shadows. I wonder if he will look at me, but he doesn't. Up close, I see the tag in his right ear—like a tag you'd put on a calf. He crosses the field toward the neighbor's house, vanishing into the tall grass.

After a little while, I start to get ready for bed. I'm still standing by the window, about to step into the shower, naked now, because there's nowhere else to stand and change in this small room. Then, a shock. Something *else* is moving out of the woods, and I hold up the cutoffs I'd been folding to cover myself, as if this animal, this wild mind, could somehow care about nakedness.

This time it's a she-bear who comes through the ferns. The male must have been her yearling cub. She's bigger, heavier, untagged—nothing managed or tame—just a life-force that trundles and pauses when she feels my gaze on her. I follow her to the next window and again she pauses, though the lights are off at this transitional hour. She stands for a moment at the top of the hill, ringed by a brittle constellation of fireflies. And then she, too, disappears into the neighbor's field.

As I fall asleep, I think of her in the greenish darkness of the woods, the blurred edge of her fur-shadow. How she caught me in a kind of vulnerability, without armor. How I felt the intensity of her presence, the opposite of a human supremacy.

After you see something once, you know where to look, how to listen—you're sensitized to see it again. A few days later, out walking and looking for birds, I hear a deep rustle at the edge of the road and freeze. An earlier version of myself might have kept walking, but I wait for the sound to resolve into whatever is coming—some animal, something big. This time, when the young bear crosses the road, I'm about fifteen feet away, and there are no walls between us. Pulse under my jaw, heart flying out of my chest. I reach up my arms to look as big as possible. The deerflies take advantage of my stillness, but I barely notice their bites. The bear looks back at me and lopes away. But something tells me to wait for his mother, not wanting to get in between them, not wanting to test the trigger of that rescue distance, that invisible tie. Sure enough, a few minutes later, she shuffles out of the roadside brush. I'm still frozen, arms overhead, fingers tingling. Up close, she's slower, more discerning. We look at each other across one whole, suspended minute, but then she, too, turns her back and walks away. And I realize the worst fear was just before the encounter began to play itself out, before we knew how we would act toward each other, before we all knew that here, at least in this one moment, our paths could cross without harm.

As I write this, I wonder if, in teaching me about birds, my father was actually teaching me how to unlearn loneliness. Telling me that though it may be impossible to step entirely outside human ways of understanding our surroundings, I should still value the longing to try. Giving me the key to a more-than-human world, the world that had comforted him after the death of his own father, who died at fifty-six.

My father was sixty when I was born. Just a few years later, he was diagnosed, although his cancer treatments were mild enough that, as a child, I didn't notice a marked change in his vitality. Still, there were many things he kept to himself. As I drifted away into teen-age years, he began to visibly sicken.

We spent less time in the woods, in the schoolhouse cabin, though when we did, we still walked at the blue hour down to the swamp where swallows dipped over the water, touching the surface like daredevil pilots. Cut hay in the air, the buzz of flies. Clusters of asters and yellow toadflax, which we called butter and eggs. Beavers swam between flooded clumps of thicket, making a dark furrow in the reflection of the sky. As the reeds in the swamp lost their defi-nition, we stood backlit at the edge of the road until the male bea-ver noticed us and clapped his tail against the surface—a warning that we'd gotten too close.

On one of our last walks through the woods, my father's foot snagged a tree root, and as he fell, his reflexes failed to catch him. Out of sheer luck, he wound up with nothing worse than shallow cuts to the face, forming a wide scab across his chin and the bridge of his nose. It was my freshman year of college, parents' weekend. Eight months later he was dead.

I didn't know then that it would take me nearly fifteen years to come back to the birds, to walk down to the vernal pools at dusk, to listen to the pull of this landscape and accept that its abundance could carry his traces. To pick up binoculars and the threads of a long-paused conversation. What he saw, what I could see.

In 2021, I join a Christmas Bird Count route in the same circle where my dad once counted with Mike. There are five of us, meeting up in the parking lot of the Audubon Center in Sharon, Connecticut, just over the line from New York State. When we arrive, it's early enough for frost to still coat the gravel as we col-lect our boots and gloves. Our route captain is a naturalist named

Bethany Sheffer, who's been kind enough to let me join, even though we've only spoken over the phone. We pile into the van, and I learn a little more about who else has shown up that day. Joshua, a college student majoring in ecology, who grew up on a farm in nearby Amenia, New York. Cheri and Jonas, a mom and son, who join for a few hours, too. Jonas looks about ten—and he's good at spotting birds. We've barely arrived at our first stop when he sees three crows on the far horizon, wings no thicker than stray eyelashes.

Joshua is clearly an ace. He's already completed a survey of the hundreds of plants that grow on the center's land and written up a report for Bethany. He's been out of the car for all of three seconds when he identifies his first bird of the count.

Meanwhile, I'm writing in my notebook and trying to make peace with a pair of borrowed binoculars—somehow, in all the packing and preparation, I'd forgotten to bring my own. Bethany, though, is in the same boat. We laugh at ourselves for a second, and she says, "That was kind of the whole deal, wasn't it," and I feel the first real grin of the day spreading across my face.

As we add new birds and tallies to our list, Bethany checks our work, peppering it with her own observations. At a pause on the route, Jonas sees a bird not five feet from the car, among the branches of a crabapple tree. *What is that*, he asks me, and I tell him it's a mockingbird—an infrequent sighting for this route at this time of year. We see two more, and Bethany wonders if catbirds and mockingbirds might be sticking around this winter, and what might be keeping them here. What we see creates new questions, observations, and I'm glad to be in this van, thinking aloud about birds.

Do species who mimic also feel compelled to collect the songs they hear in a lifetime? Could a mockingbird keep alive the song of a bird that's extinct? Far from the woods of rural Connecticut, there's at least one mimic who does retain and transmit the sounds of places they've known. According to ornithologist Ana Dalziell, Australian lyrebirds are "archivists of soundscapes." When a population was transplanted from Australia to Tasmania, they continued to mimic species and sounds from their previous habitat for several generations. Dalziell sees this kind of memory as "compelling proof of cultural transmission, one generation passing on knowledge to the next."

We keep the windows open as we drive around the back roads, and the cold wind carries the smell of pines and hemlocks, the knocking of woodpeckers and the clicking of branches. Bethany somehow manages to keep her eyes on both the road and the birds, pulling over to let other cars pass. As we drive through an uncut meadow, a hawk hovers over the soft tips of the grass, drifting sideways on the wind like a ripple in the body of a wave. Bethany jumps out of the car—it's a harrier, coasting for a meal.

After that, Jonas and Cheri need to get going, but Jonas drags his feet. He's riveted, caught in a net of observations and questions. Those of us who are left work in bursts—little conversations, flutters of activity, and quiet moments when we listen to the landscape. It surprises me how quickly these silences become companionable.

From the back seat, I learn to lean toward the window and spot birds by looking straight up. In a tall stand of trees near a farm, I call softly for Bethany to stop the car. There's a bald eagle perched right above us, eating a chicken carcass stolen from the coop. As the van door slides open, he drops it, and Joshua points out the scraggly remains, hidden in a tangle of Virginia creeper. Bird count data shows that bald eagle numbers have grown substantially since Rachel Carson's *Silent Spring* called attention to DDT.

When we pause for lunch, I ask Joshua how he became interested in birding, but he pushes back a little at the term. For someone who grew up on a nearby farm, he tells me, knowing the names of birds and plants seems like second nature. I suspect he's being modest, but he also has a point. He's been awake to this landscape his whole life. Which reminds me that what we're doing out here is more than just observing birds for stats or for human enjoyment. Surveying a population isn't quite the same as checking off as many boxes as you can. We're not just casually observing—we're adding small pieces to a shifting picture, tending a long archive of encounters.

The following year, Mike lets me join his route, which he and a friend (also named Mike) have been tallying for forty-six years. At dawn, we're in the parking lot of a marina, watching the hillsides turn pink across the lake. Herring gulls circle, white specks on the dark water. Though I stayed up late studying ducks, I worry the Mikes will be impatient with all the things I still don't know. Instead, we walk around the lake, cracking up when a faraway great blue heron turns out, on closer inspection, to be an Adirondack chair perched in the reeds. A young eagle skims over our heads, diving into a flock of mergansers. By late morning, we're trespassing, moving through dense thickets off someone's driveway. *I'm just going to look in here to find the hermit thrush*, Mike says, as if he were popping in to run an errand.

Our last stop is at a farm in a valley, where the afternoon sun warms us as it dips toward the hills. It's sheltered here, out of the wind, and there are sparrows everywhere. The two men are walking up the road, talking companionably about septic tanks. Every few feet, there's something. But in a tree over the corncrib, a pale blaze stands out against the sky—a perching bird of prey, with a blip of tail visible below the branch. Mike sets up the scope so we can all look closer, running through the subtle differences between one faraway hawk and another. I'm waiting for him to identify it but he passes me the viewfinder instead. *Your call.* I tell him it's a Cooper's hawk and he nods. *You've got your father in you,* he says.

In bird-watching, there is something called a life list—a collection of every species a person has ever encountered. The list reveals the range of habitats, how far someone went out of their way to find the rare or the shy, whether they searched for birds on their travels.

What it doesn't tell you is how many times someone walked the same patch of woods, how many hours they spent watching common species, if they took the time to understand their habits. I don't know if my father kept a life list. I've never been able to find one. But if he did, I would want it to tell me more than the story of a life defined by its end point. I would want it to include the ways we pass through these places and carry them with us, how they entangle us with the whole mess of creatures we love. I want the branchings of pathways he crossed and—for better or worse—the landscapes that imprinted themselves: the Bedfordshire fields; Japan, as a young Air Force conscript after the bombing of Hiroshima; California in the 1970s; the highways of Texas and the rural roads of Connecticut's northwest corner. The time he pointed out the gradient of an indigo bunting, the exact color of a darkening sky. Or the time a bobcat crossed the meadow while he and my mother were sleeping, and I memorized the markings so I could describe them for him.

The time I caught a first trout, how I held it without wetting my hands—how I wanted to release her, and how if I had, I would have left a human handprint in the membrane on her scales. How we ate that fish, how capably he pulled the bone out of the meat.

How he showed me a clearing where a tornado touched down, ripping the trees out in a circle, making a ring of vertical roots in the air.

How the woods looked after a rain—tiny beads of water balanced along canes of bramble—sharp glints where the sun dropped through—

How our cat escaped, how we played the sound of her feeder, how coyotes howled back from the hills—

How I woke to find that a firefly had come inside, pulsing against the ceiling, making the whole schoolhouse its jar—

The sky, just after a storm, and the vertigo of binoculars—

The cold front from the west and the birds coasting on it, a swarm in the tangle of bittersweet—

The tree of heaven whose roots let rain into our cellar,

The fast car and the woodchuck dead in the road, broken tooth pierced through its tongue,

The tang of marsh, caught on the roof of the palette,

The plaque on a fence post by the Cornwall river, warning pregnant women not to eat the catch,

How blue the sky looks through a vulture's scraggle of wings,

All the thorns my father pruned on blood thinners, how they marbled the veins under the skin of his hands—

The things he taught me, how they bled into my own observations—

The time I stood in the river at dusk as tree swallows circled. How the cars drove over the covered bridge without seeing the heron perched on the roof—

The shadow of a fox touching the grass outside the library,

The gap between the jet bridge and the plane that let in a strip of humid air,

The taste of dirt, the taste of river water,

The ring around the moon and the death of a tardigrade, and the span of a horseshoe's shell,

The ground-truth of a life, the silence of lost data—

How the field cracks open, what rises through the stream in the rain,

The screen door that slams after the undertaker, the house that never again feels like a home—

A bear down the trail that I hoped hadn't seen me, how I turned and left him there—

The dust at Love Canal, the thin coating, dull on the hood of the car

The taste of fear, the taste of failure

The cherry I ate, furtively, from a tree by the poisoned river

How the nightjar kept calling, how she fed in the moonlight, what she saw after I fell asleep

How the world continues, how the catbird sings what he remembers—

The birds I know and the birds I've never seen.

CBC 2022
12.18.2022

Twin Lakes - Sharon
w/ Mike Root
Mike Redmond

- ✓ hooded mergansers - 9, 82
- ✓ eastern bluebirds - 3, 2, 5, 3
- ✓ herring gull - 6, 10, 7
- ✓ American crow - 2, 6, 2, 6
- ✓ Black-capped chickadee - 2, 4, 17, 2, 2, 1, 1
- ✓ Blue Jay - 1, 2, 1, 1, 3
- ✓ Hairy woodpecker - 2, 1, 1
- ✓ tufted titmouse - 3, 2, 4
- ✓ white-breasted nuthatch - 1, 6, 1
- ✓ Red Bellied woodpecker - 1, 1, 1, 1, 1
- ✓ cardinal - 2, 6, 1, 2, 1
- ✓ downy woodpecker - 1, 2, 1, 2
- ✓ hermit thrush - 6
- ✓ winter wren - 1
- ✓ Carolina wren - 1, 1, 1
- ✓ dark eyed junco - 5, 3, 8, 10, 8
- ✓ house finch - 2
- ✓ white-throated sparrow - 5, 1
- ✓ red-breasted nuthatch - 6
- ✓ American Robin - 12, 2, 3
- ✓ Yellow Bellied Sapsucker - 1
- ✓ Great-horned owl - 4
- ✓ common goldeneye - 1
- ✓ common merganser - 2, 1
- ✓ belted kingfisher - 1, 2
- ✓ european starling - 9, 5, 7
- ✓ red tailed hawk - 2, 2
- ✓ bald eagle - 1
- ✓ house sparrows - 30, 26, 12
- ✓ Canada geese - 21, 6
- ✓ mallard - 3, 1
- ✓ black duck - 2
- ✓ cooper's hawk - 1
- ✓ sharp-shinned hawk - 1
- ✓ northern mockingbird - 3
- ✓ mourning dove - 13
- ✓ turkey - 10

Notes

Epigraphs

"It is a hallmark . . . alone": Robin Wall Kimmerer, "White Pine," *The Mind of Plants: Narratives of Vegetal Intelligence,* John C. Ryan, Patrícia Vieira, and Monica Gagliano, eds. (Synergetic Press, 2021), 425.

"You hold a face . . . the world": Anne Boyer, "Erotology," *A Handbook of Disappointed Fate* (Ugly Duckling Presse, 2018), 85.

1. Lost Lake

5 **exist outside this framework:** my thinking about landscapes has been informed by Daegan Miller's excellent *This Radical Land: A Natural History of American Dissent* (University of Chicago Press, 2018); and *Landscape and Power,* W. J. T. Mitchell, ed. (University of Chicago Press, 2002). Concerning the ways remembered places inform and shape written work, I've looked to Toni Morrison's classic essay "The Site of Memory," in *Inventing the Truth: The Art and Craft of Memoir,* William Zinsser, ed. (Houghton Mifflin, 1995).

5 **"follow the landscape . . . into being":** Miller, *This Radical Land,* 6.

7 **the town historian:** with thanks to Joel Helander and Nona Bloomer for fielding my questions.

7 **"by, for, and of ourselves," "the Eremocene . . . Loneliness":** E. O. Wilson, *Half-Earth: Our Planet's Fight for Life* (Liveright, 2016), 20.

8 **"I have frequent . . . earth":** Robert Macfarlane, interviewed by Diane Ackerman, *Conjunctions: 73: Earth Elegies,* fall 2019, https://www.conjunctions.com/print/article/robert-macfarlane-c73.

9 "fall into the space . . . it is love": Hanif Abdurraquib, "The Year in Living Alone," *Hazlitt*, December 8, 2017, https://hazlitt.net/feature/year-living-alone.

10 "I am not sure . . . believe I have learned": Frieda Fromm-Reichmann, "Loneliness," *Psychiatry*, 22:1, February 1, 1959, 1.

11 "Loneliness seems to be . . . everything to avoid it": Fromm-Reichmann, "Loneliness."

11 "I didn't want . . . grow older on a web": Erica Berry, *Wolfish: Wolf, Self, and the Stories We Tell About Fear* (Flatiron Books, 2023), 321.

12 the sea between a brace of islands: Nancy S. Seasholes, *Gaining Ground: A History of Landmaking in Boston* (MIT Press, 2003), 355.

12 Wood Island: Seasholes, *Gaining Ground*, 105.

12 "'Floods' is the word . . . where it was": Morrison, "The Site of Memory," 99.

13 "As our human . . . more lonely": Robin Wall Kimmerer, *Braiding Sweetgrass: Indigenous Wisdom, Scientific Knowledge, and the Teachings of Plants* (Milkweed Editions, 2013), 208.

13 "citizen of longing": Boyer, "Erotology," 85.

14 twenty-four hours counting birds: for data on the Christmas Bird Count, see https://www.audubon.org/conservation/science/christmas-bird-count.

2. Extremotolerance

17 from the tallest of the Himalayas: Pritam Dey and Krishnendu Mondal, "Tardigrada of Indian Himalaya," in Kailash Chandra et al., *Faunal Diversity of Indian Himalaya* (Zoological Survey of India, 2018), 779.

17 can also withstand intense forms of harshness: Diane R. Nelson, "Current Status of the Tardigrada: Evolution and Ecology," *Integrative and Comparative Biology*, 42:3, July 1, 2002, 652–659, https://doi.org/10.1093/icb/42.3.652.

18 Humans have irradiated . . . outer space: K. Ingeman Jönsson et al., "Tardigrades Survive Exposure to Space in Low Earth Orbit," *Current Biology*, 18:17, September 9, 2008, 729–731, https://doi.org/10.1016/j.cub.2008.06.048.

18 **outlast us on this planet:** Ben Guarino, "These Animals Can Survive Until the End of the Earth, Astrophysicists Say," *Washington Post*, July 14, 2017.

18 **can also fly:** Matthew Mogle et al., "Evidence of Avian-Mediated Long Distance Dispersal in American Tardigrades," *PeerJ*, July 4, 2018, https:// peerj.com/articles/5035/.

18 **crashed on the moon:** Daniel Oberhaus, "A Crashed Israeli Lunar Lander Spilled Tardigrades on the Moon," *Wired*, August 5, 2019. On epoxy resin, see also Nova Spivack, "The Lunar Library™," document for the Arch Mission Foundation, April 22, 2019, 71.

19 **"Lunar Library™":** Spivack, "The Lunar Library™," 1.

19 **"for the first 24 hours . . . significant":** Oberhaus, "A Crashed Israeli Lunar Lander."

19 **"Humanity's Backup Plan":** This tag line has been removed, but it was the first text on the Arch Mission Foundation's home page, https://www. archmission.org/ (accessed via the Internet Archive, February 2, 2019).

19 **"The Billion Year Archive":** Spivack, "The Lunar Library™," 8. See also the Arch Mission Foundation's "Billion Year Archive": https://www .archmission.org/billion-year-archive.

19 **"a cherry red Tesla Roadster":** Spivack, "The Lunar Library™," 9.

20 **"It will survive . . . possible":** Helen Macdonald, *Vesper Flights* (Grove Press, 2020), 96.

20 **The project was designed:** Matt Kenyon, *Tardigotchi*, https://www .swamp.nu/tardigotchi.

21 **"I come as a guest / entering my own life":** Mary Oppen, *Meaning a Life* (New Directions, 2020), 253.

21 **a tiny parasite:** Louis H. du Preez and Itumeleng A. Moeng, "Additional Morphological Information on *Oculotrema Hippopotami* Stunkard, 1924 (Monogenea: Polystomatidae) Parasitic on the African Hippopotamus," *African Zoology*, 39:2, 2004, 225–233, https://doi.org/10.1080/15627020 .2004.11657219.

22 **"'deep-time' communication":** for an overview of this discipline, see Thomas A. Sebeok, "Communication Measures to Bridge Ten Millennia,"

US Department of Energy, April 1984. https://doi.org/10.2172/6705990. See also Jon Lomberg, "A Portrait of Humanity," on his website: https://www.jonlomberg.com/articles/a_portrait_of_humanity.html.

22 **"*Eureka!* moment," "My feelings as a 27 year old woman . . . fear of death":** NASA Science, "Voyager, the Love Story," April 28, 2011, https://science.nasa.gov/science-news/science-at-nasa/2011/28apr_voyager2.

23 **"the world's largest . . . seed samples":** "Major Seed Deposit at the Svalbard Global Seed Vault, Longyearbyen," Crop Trust Resource Library, February 25, 2020.

23 **permafrost thawed and caused a flood:** Damian Carrington, "Arctic Stronghold of World's Seeds Flooded After Permafrost Melts," *Guardian*, May 19, 2017.

23 **Lomberg helped draft warning signs:** Kathleen M. Trauth et al., "Expert Judgment on Markers to Deter Inadvertent Human Intrusion into the Waste Isolation Pilot Plant," Sandia National Laboratories, November 1993, Appendix G, 3. See also Samuel Gilbert, "The Man Who Helped Design a 10,000-Year Nuclear Waste Site Marker," *VICE*, April 26, 2018.

23 **the Withdrawal:** the name is taken from the Land Withdrawal Act that created the area. See Geoff Manaugh and Nicola Twilley, *Until Proven Safe: The History and Future of Quarantine* (New York: Farrar, Straus and Giroux, 2021), 244.

23 **Indigenous inhabitants . . . exposure hazards:** see the Navajo Nation testimony before Congress on the legacy damage of uranium mining in the Southwest, "Hearing on the Health and Environmental Impacts of Uranium Contamination in the Navajo Nation," House Hearing, 110th Congress, October 23, 2007, 9. See also WIPP, "Comment Response Document," September 1997.

24 *The Scream*: Trauth, "Expert Judgment," Appendix F, figure 4.5-4.

24 **cats that would change color, "atomic priesthood":** Manaugh and Twilley, *Until Proven Safe*, 260–261.

24 **"this place is not . . . valued is here":** Trauth, "Expert Judgment," Appendix F, 49.

24 **damage suppressor:** Nathan Tauger and Victoria Gill, "Survival Secret of 'Earth's Hardiest Animal' Revealed," *BBC News*, September 20, 2016. See also Takuma Hashimoto et al., "Extremotolerant Tardigrade Genome

and Improved Radiotolerance of Human Cultured Cells by Tardigrade-Unique Protein," *Nature Communications*, September 20, 2016, https://doi.org/10.1038/ncomms12808.

25 **"Facts are perceptions of surfaces," "words are widows of thought":** Susan Howe, *The Quarry* (New Directions, 2015), 112, 22.

25 **tardigrades exposed to the hard vacuum of space survived:** Jönsson, "Tardigrades Survive."

26 **believed in an afterlife:** Ann Druyan, "Ann Druyan Talks About Science, Religion, Wonder, Awe . . . and Carl Sagan," *Skeptical Enquirer*, 27:6, November–December, 2003, 30.

3. Flat-Earthers

28 **Mcity was a field, flat people:** for an overview of the facility, see https://mcity.umich.edu/our-work/mcity-test-facility/.

28 **step off a curb:** see the simulated pedestrian in this *Quartz* video of Mcity, https://www.youtube.com/watch?v=pqfGL506ezU.

30 **By Michigan law:** according to Michigan.gov, "If you are hurt in an auto accident, this [personal injury projection] part of your no-fault policy will pay all reasonably necessary medical expenses with no maximum limit." In theory, this required auto insurance could pay the patient and the hospital more than (for example) a health plan that covers only a percentage or requires a deductible.

31 **quarter of Pfizer's sales:** over the course of a decade. See Duff Wilson, "Facing Generic Lipitor Rivals, Lipitor Battles to Protect Its Cash Cow," *New York Times*, November 29, 2011.

31 **a study called ILLUMINATE . . . facility:** John LaMattina, "A Story of Devastation and Rebirth: The Former Pfizer Research Labs in Ann Arbor," *Forbes*, June 11, 2018.

33 **Elaine Herzberg was killed by a self-driving car:** "Collision Between Vehicle Controlled by Developmental Automated Driving System and Pedestrian, Tempe, Arizona, March 18, 2018," Highway Accident Report, National Transportation Safety Board (NTSB), November 19, 2019, v.

33 **one employee could perform both functions:** NTSB, "Collision Between," 45.

33 **"operators' automation complacency"**: NTSB, "Collision Between," 58.

33 **Uber had not been required:** NTSB, "Collision Between," 54–55. Arizona has since revised its policies. Experts have also pointed out that a large number of disengagements could be a sign of an attentive backup driver—so while this metric should be tracked, a large number of disengagements doesn't always reflect poor design.

33 **"Move Fast and Break Things":** see this thread on the Y Combinator forum (some of the comments are extremely cruel): https://news .ycombinator.com/item?id=21463903.

34 **In her free time:** see Elaine Herzberg's obituary, https://www.findagrave .com/memorial/188210426/elaine-marie-herzberg.

34 **grandchildren and a daughter:** see the comments on "The Untold Story of Elaine Herzberg," America Friends Service Committee Arizona, May 14, 2018, https://afscarizona.org/2018/05/14/the-untold-story-of-elaine -herzberg/.

34 **"edge case," "the car recognized":** NTSB, "Collision Between," 15–16.

35 **half its forests . . . grasslands:** for a conservation overview in Michigan, see "Michigan Conservation Summary," LandScope America, http:// www.landscope.org/michigan/overview/. See also M. A. Kost, "Natural Community Abstract for Mesic Prairie," Michigan Natural Features Inventory, 2004, 3.

35 **forty-nine acres of old-growth pine:** Dustin Dwyer, "From Wilderness to Wasteland: How the Destruction of Michigan's Forests Shaped Our State," Michigan Radio, October 17, 2018.

35 **"renaming fish . . . ventures":** Eileen Crist, "On the Poverty of Our Nomenclature," *Environmental Humanities*, 3:1, May 1, 2013, 144.

37 **GPS adopter even went on NPR:** interview with Emily Yoffe, "Stories of GPS Directions Gone Wrong," NPR, August 12, 2009.

37 **In Leonia, New Jersey:** Lisa W. Foderaro, "Navigation Apps Are Turning Quiet Neighborhoods into Traffic Nightmares," *New York Times*, December 24, 2017.

38 **"The memory . . . amnesia of what is," "It is the dimension . . . found":** Robert Smithson, "Incidents of Mirror-Travel in the Yucatan," *Artforum*, September 1969.

39 **"the great thinning," "As we come . . . the earth":** Michael McCarthy, *The Moth Snowstorm: Nature and Joy* (New York Review Books, 2015), 99, 14.

39 **the *Oxford Junior Dictionary*:** Alison Flood, "Oxford Junior Dictionary's Replacement of 'Natural' Words with 21st-Century Terms Sparks Outcry," *Guardian*, January 13, 2015. Writer Robert Macfarlane has created collaborations with artists and songwriters to celebrate the words that were taken out of the dictionary, notably, with Jackie Morris, *The Lost Words: A Spell Book* (Hamish Hamilton, 2017).

40 **understanding of what's "normal" becomes thinner:** This phenomenon is also called shifting baseline syndrome. See Masashi Soga and Kevin J. Gaston, "Shifting Baseline Syndrome: Causes, Consequences, and Implications," *Frontiers in Ecology and the Environment*, 16:4, May 2018, https://doi.org/10.1002/fee.1794.

4. Cancerine

45 **some 445 to 475 million years:** Deborah Cramer, *The Narrow Edge: A Tiny Bird, an Ancient Crab, and an Epic Journey* (Yale University Press, 2015), 76.

46 **mature horseshoe crabs accumulate:** Dave Grant, "Living on *Limulus*," in John T. Tanacredi et al., eds., *Limulus in the Limelight: A Species 350 Million Years in the Making and in Peril?* (Springer, 2001). Grant's drawings of horseshoe crab fouling are also here: https://www.horseshoecrab.org /nh/eco.html.

46 **"moving menagerie":** Grant, "Living on *Limulus*," 136.

47 **"Grant that Odysseus . . . house":** Homer, *The Odyssey*, Emily Wilson, trans. (W. W. Norton, 2018), 257.

48 **as well by moonlight:** Robert Barlow and Maureen K. Powers, "Seeing at Night and Finding Mates: The Role of Vision," in Carl N. Shuster et al., eds., *The American Horseshoe Crab* (Harvard University Press, 2003), 91, 94.

48 **a strong circadian rhythm:** Barlow and Powers, "Seeing at Night," 91.

48 **"To understand the shore . . . foothold":** Rachel Carson, *The Rocky Coast* (Houghton Mifflin, 1955), ix.

48 **Vision researcher Robert Barlow:** Barlow and Powers, "Seeing at Night," 95.

49   "To understand . . . its relations": Carson, *The Rocky Coast*, ix–x.

49   navigate by the slope of the beach: Jane Brockmann, "Nesting Behavior: A Shoreline Phenomenon," in Shuster, *The American Horseshoe Crab*, 45.

50   feed on *limulus* eggs: for an excellent account of the relationship between shorebirds and horseshoe crabs, see Cramer, *The Narrow Edge*.

50   depleted Delaware's soil: William H. Williams, *Man and Nature in Delaware: An Environmental History of the First State* (Delaware Heritage Press, 2008), 145.

50   "Under such a system . . . certain": William Huffington, quoted in Williams, *Man and Nature*.

50   black oaks: Williams, *Man and Nature*, 147.

50   they tried importing: Williams, *Man and Nature*, 149.

51   sustainable, Indigenous practices: Gary Kreamer and Stewart Michels, "History of Horseshoe Crab Harvest on Delaware Bay," in John T. Tanacredi, *Biology and Conservation of Horseshoe Crabs* (Springer Verlag, 2009), 302–304.

51   crab fertilizer had caught on: Carl N. Shuster, "King Crab Fertilizer: A Once Thriving Delaware Bay Industry," in his book *The American Horseshoe Crab*, 348. See also Cramer's account of the first Cancerine factory, and speculation in *The Narrow Edge*, 64.

51   like a fieldstone wall: see images in Kreamer and Michels, "History of Horseshoe Crab Harvest," 302–304. (Many of these are also available through the Delaware Public Archives.)

52   Cancerine: "King-Crabs and the Manufacture of Cancerine," *Scientific American*, June 5, 1869.

52   A cancer means a crab: Though many scholars have tried to locate the metaphorical leap from the creature to the disease, we still don't know quite how the concepts first became tethered. One theory suggests that an ancient Greek doctor thought the pinch of a crab resembled the pain of a malignant tumor.

52   "Capitalist economics . . . timescales": Timothy Morton, *Dark Ecology: For a Logic of Future Coexistence* (Columbia University Press, 2016), 35.

52 **at minimum fifty to one hundred million crabs:** this is a conservative estimate, based on the numbers of harvested crabs between 1870 and 1920. See Shuster, "King Crab Fertilizer," 356–357, and Kreamer and Michels, "History of Horseshoe Crab Harvest," 306.

53 **"Sachem's Head":** there are several sources for the origin of this name, including Davenport's letter. See Richard Davenport to Hugh Peter, c. July 17, 1637, Winthrop Family Papers, Massachusetts Historical Society. This information is repeated in John Winthrop's journal: "Mr. Stoughton, with about eighty of the English, sailed to the west in pursuit of Sassacus, etc. At Quinepiack [now New Haven], they killed six and took two. At a head of land a little short they beheaded two sachems; whereupon they called the place Sachem's Head," *The Journal of John Winthrop, 1630–1649* (Harvard University Press, 1996), 125. With gratitude to Hazel Carby for sharing her research on the history of the name, which she also discusses in her essay on CRT and the history of Guilford, Connecticut, "We Must Burn Them," *London Review of Books*, 44:10, May 26, 2022, https://www.lrb.co.uk/the-paper/v44/n10/hazel-v.-carby/we-must-burn-them.

53 **the story of the name had shifted:** see Bernard Christian Steiner's accounting of the papers of Ralph Dunning Smyth (also spelled Smith), *A History of the Plantation of Menunkatuck and of the Original Town of Guilford, Connecticut: Comprising the Present Towns of Guilford and Madison* (Steiner, 1897), 207–208.

54 **"a few of the Connecticut soldiers," "Uncas himself . . . arrow":** Steiner, *A History*. Smyth's earlier manuscript reads "some English soldiers."

54 **"stories . . . homelands":** Jean M. O'Brien, *Firsting and Lasting: Writing Indians out of Existence in New England* (University of Minnesota Press, 2010), 102.

54 **"ten thousand years . . . recorded history," "O.K. with that":** Penelope Green, "The Monoliths Next Door," *New York Times*, October 13, 2005, https://www.nytimes.com/2005/10/13/garden/the-monoliths-next-door.html.

55 **fertilizer tapered off:** Shuster, "King Crab Fertilizer," 341.

55 **Fritz Haber:** see the 1918 rationale for the Nobel Prize in Chemistry at https://www.nobelprize.org/prizes/chemistry/1918/haber/facts/. See also Benjamín Labatut's engaging (very lightly fictionalized) account of Haber

in his book *When We Cease to Understand the World*, Adrian Nathan West, trans. (Pushkin Press, 2020).

56 **"an equivalent death . . . land":** Elmer Wilgrid Cotton, quoted in Marion Girard, *A Strange and Formidable Weapon: British Responses to World War I Poison Gas* (University of Nebraska Press, 2008), 1.

56 **minute amounts of gold:** Daniel Charles, *Master Mind: The Rise and Fall of Fritz Haber, the Nobel Laureate Who Launched the Age of Chemical Warfare* (Ecco, 2005), 199.

56 **tiny amounts of gram-negative bacteria, "burning bodies," live rabbits:** for an excellent account of the development and processes that led to medical testing with horseshoe crab blood, see William Sargent, *Crab Wars: A Tale of Horseshoe Crabs, Ecology, and Human Health*, 2nd ed. (Brandeis University Press, 2022), 36–38.

56 **immune system:** Jordan Krisfalusi-Gannon et al., "The Role of Horseshoe Crabs in the Biomedical Industry and Recent Trends Impacting Species Sustainability," *Frontiers in Marine Science*, vol. 5, June 5, 2018, https://doi .org/10.3389/fmars.2018.00185.

57 **billions of doses:** James Gorman, "Tests for Coronavirus Vaccine Need This Ingredient: Horseshoe Crabs," *New York Times*, June 3, 2020.

57 **"It is crazy making . . . pandemic":** Gorman, "Tests for Coronavirus Vaccine."

59 **don't die alone:** Grant, "Living on *Limulus*," 136.

60 **scrub everything off:** Latif Nasser, "Baby Blue Blood Drive," *Radiolab*, July 23, 2020, https://radiolab.org/podcast/baby-blue-blood-drive /transcript.

60 **10 to 30 percent of individuals die:** see Krisfalusi-Gannon, "The Role of Horseshoe Crabs," and A. S. Leschen and S. J. Correia, "Mortality in Female Horseshoe Crabs (*Limulus polyphemus*) from Biomedical Bleeding and Handling: Implications for Fisheries Management," *Marine and Freshwater Behaviour and Physiology*, 43:2, April 2010, http://dx.doi .org/10.1080/10236241003786873.

61 **right back at fertilizer-harvest levels:** Cramer, *The Narrow Edge*, 107.

61 **"Where is memory . . . diminished":** Cramer, *The Narrow Edge*, 107.

61   The **"stock status . . . poor"**: Atlantic States Marine Fisheries Commission, "2019 Horseshoe Crab Benchmark Stock Assessment Peer Review Report," 15. (Note that Long Island Sound is considered part of the New York region.)

61   **"with the optimism . . . proven"**: Sherwin B. Nuland, *How We Die: Reflections on Life's Final Chapter* (Random House, 1994), 220–221.

62   **"the capacity . . . end"**: Anne Boyer, *The Undying: Pain, Vulnerability, Mortality, Medicine, Art, Time, Dreams, Data, Exhaustion, Cancer, and Care* (Farrar, Straus and Giroux, 2019), 249.

63   **"Instead of a vigil . . . remembrance"**: Adam Zagajewski, "A Quick Poem," Clare Cavanagh, trans., in *Without End: New and Selected Poems* (Farrar, Straus and Giroux, 2002), 213.

65   **eaten up the places where they once spawned:** Jennifer Mattei, interview with the author, May 5, 2022. See also Mark Beekey and Jennifer Mattei, "The Mismanagement of *Limulus polyphemus* in Long Island Sound, U.S.A.: What Are the Characteristics of a Population in Decline?," in Ruth H. Carmichael et al., eds., *Changing Global Perspectives on Horseshoe Crab Biology, Conservation and Management* (Springer, 2015).

65   **Project Limulus:** this community science horseshoe crab project was run by Mattei before she died, in 2023. For more information, see https://www.sacredheart.edu/academics/colleges-schools/college-of-arts-sciences/departments/biology/project-limulus/.

5. *Safer Skies for All Who Fly*

71   **"heavy concentrations":** Niagara Frontier Transportation Authority, "Environmental Overview" in *Buffalo Niagara International Airport Sustainable Master Plan Update*, 6.

71   **"on top of upper surface . . . sharp curve":** "Diaries and Notebooks: 1905, Wilbur Wright," Manuscript Division, Library of Congress, https://www.loc.gov/item/wright002244/.

71   **"Birds, which had been practicing . . . airspace":** Richard Dolbeer, "The History of Wildlife Strikes and Management at Airports," in Travis DeVault et al., eds., *Wildlife in Airport Environments: Preventing Animal-Aircraft Collisions Through Science-Based Management,* (Johns Hopkins University Press, 2013), 1.

71 **15,556 bird strikes:** Richard Dolbeer et al., "Wildlife Strikes to Civil Aircraft in the United States, 1990–2021," Federal Aviation Administration National Wildlife Strike Database Serial Report no. 28, June 2022, v.

72 **rooster booster or chicken gun:** Pell Kangas and George L. Pigman, "Development of Aircraft Windshields to Resist Impact with Birds in Flight," Civil Aeronautics Administration, February 1950, 2–3. (The technical term is "flight-impact simulator.")

72 **an online database of airplane wildlife strikes:** https://wildlife.faa.gov /home.

73 **struck as they dive:** Travis DeVault, interview with the author, May 26, 2022. See also his paper on the subject, with Glen E. Bernhardt et al., "Fatal Injuries to Birds from Collisions with Aircraft Reveal Anti-Predator Behaviours," *International Journal of Avian Science*, 152:4, August 5, 2010, https://doi.org/10.1111/j.1474-919X.2010.01043.x.

73 **"a disturbing reminder . . . sky":** Thom Patterson, "Preventing another 'Miracle on the Hudson' Emergency," *CNN*, September 12, 2016, quoted in Christopher Schaberg, *Airportness: The Nature of Flight* (Bloomsbury, 2017), 76–77.

73 **"confounding as-if epiphany . . . news":** Schaberg, *Airportness*, 77.

74 **earthworms don't crawl on the tarmac:** Navjot S. Sodhi, "Competition in the Air: Birds vs. Aircraft," *The Auk*, 119:3, 592.

74 **Shooting geese with paintball guns:** Laura Francoeur, interview with CNN, online at the Port Authority of New York and New Jersey blog, *PORTfolio*, August 25, 2017, https://portfolio.panynj.gov/2017/08/25 /laura-francoeurs-job-is-for-the-birds-and-the-terrapins/.

74 **predator in the form of an airport biologist:** DeVault, interview with the author.

74 **"zero tolerance policy" for geese:** Simon Akam, "For Culprits in Miracle on Hudson, the Flip Side of Glory," *New York Times*, October 2, 2009, https://www.nytimes.com/2009/10/03/nyregion/03geese.html.

74 **coated goose eggs in corn oil:** "Egg Oil: An Avian Population Control Tool," US Department of Agriculture Wildlife Services, April 2001.

75 **only a tiny fraction of resident species:** "Environmental Assessment: Wildlife Hazard Reduction: John F. Kennedy International Airport,"

US Department of Agriculture and Animal and Plant Health Inspection Service, March 2020, 45.

75 **further analysis of the goose feathers:** Peter P. Marra, Carla Dove, et al., "Migratory Canada Geese Cause Crash of US Airways Flight 1549," *Frontiers in Ecology and the Environment*, 7:6, August 2009, 297–301. https://doi.org/10.1890/090066.

77 **The data the Feather Lab gathers:** the Feather Identification Lab also partners with the Federal Aviation Administration and the US Military, and provides identification data for its records. Bird strike reporting is mandatory for military pilots.

78 **A robust list of bird strikes and subsequent quotes from Dove, unless otherwise noted:** Carla Dove, interview with the author, April 1, 2022.

79 **"safety investigation material":** see the snarge submission form at https://www.faa.gov/airports/airport_safety/wildlife/smithsonian.

80 **barbules . . . nodes like bells:** Carla Dove and Sandra Koch, "Microscopy of Feathers: A Practical Guide for Forensic Feather Identification," *The Microscope*, 59:2, 2011, 66–68.

82 **"It is hard to imagine . . . magnificent raptors":** Norman Smith, "A Decade of Snowy Owls at Logan Airport," *Bird Observer*, 22:1, 1994. See also these more recent updates to his work: https://www.youtube.com/watch?v=hzWEWdKeIWc.

83 **samples their blood:** for more information on snowy owls absorbing toxins from eating poisoned rodents, see Amanda McGowan, "Meet the Man Who Saves Snowy Owls from Logan Airport," WGBH, April 19, 2018, https://www.wgbh.org/news/2018/04/19/life-science/meet-man-who-saves-snowy-owls-logan-airport.

84 **first-stage turbine blades:** Strike Report Confirmation, December 3, 2018, Feather Identification Lab archive, with thanks to Carla Dove.

85 **drop by about 30 percent:** Dove, interview with the author. See also Dolbeer, "Wildlife Strikes to Civil Aircraft."

87 **"to keep birds . . . live, too":** Carla Dove, in-person interview, September 8, 2022.

89 **Birds perceive much more:** Benjamin Van Doren, interview with the author, April 7, 2022.

89 **Flying creatures often aren't territorial:** Robert H. Diehl et al., "Extending the Habitat Concept to the Airspace," in Philip B. Chilson et al., eds., *Aeroecology* (Springer, 2017), 52.

89 **zone of light-polluted air and subsequent quotes from Van Doren in chapter:** Van Doren, interview with the author. See also his paper with Kyle Horton et al., "High-Intensity Urban Light Installation Dramatically Alters Nocturnal Bird Migration," *Proceedings of the National Academy of Sciences*, 114:42, October 2, 2017.

89 **BirdCast:** for information on radar and ground-truthing for migrating birds, see BirdCast's Weather Surveillance and Bird Migration Primer, https://birdcast.info/about/weather-surveillance-radar-and-bird -migration-primer/.

90 **how airborne creatures perceive disruptions to their world:** for an overview of considerations in aerial habitats, see Diehl, "Extending the Habitat Concept," 49–50.

6. Vertical Time

95 **"the horizontal line . . . places":** Berger, *And Our Faces, My Heart, Brief as Photos* (Pantheon, 1984), 56. I slightly prefer the version of this inter-section as he described it later in life, in the documentary *The Seasons in Quincy: Four Portraits of John Berger*, Tilda Swinton, Colin MacCabe, and Christopher Roth, 2016.

96 **"My view of time . . . death":** Berger, *And Our Faces*, 15.

96 **pronghorn 700031A:** Ben Guarino, "Safe Passages," *Washington Post*, March 18, 2020, https://www.washingtonpost.com/graphics/2020 /climate-solutions/wyoming-wildlife-corridor/.

96 **pronghorn don't like to jump fences:** Wenjing Xu et al., "Barrier Behaviour Analysis (BaBA) Reveals Extensive Effects of Fencing on Wide-Ranging Ungulates," *Journal of Applied Ecology*, 58:4, April 2021, 690–698. https://doi.org/10.1111/1365-2664.13806.

97 **far longer than the highways:** see William J. Rudd et al., *Wild Migrations: Atlas of Wyoming's Ungulates* (Oregon State University Press, 2018), 36. Greg Nickerson contributed writing for this page of the atlas.

97 **"green wave":** Guarino, "Safe Passages." See also Jerod A. Merkle et al., "Large Herbivores Surf Waves of Green-Up During Spring," *Proceedings of*

the Royal Society B, 283:1833, June 29, 2016, https://doi.org/10.1098/rspb
.2016.0456.

97   **"You road I enter upon . . . here"**: Walt Whitman, "Song of the Open
Road," from *Leaves of Grass* (David McKay, 1900), 169.

98   **other species usually wind up dead**: For background on the dis-
parity between impacts to humans and wildlife, see Federal Highway
Administration, "Wildlife-Vehicle Collision Reduction Study: Report
to Congress," August 2008, 7–9.

99   **trails that were built by Indigenous people**: see "Route 66: Sharing
Our History: Hispanic Legacies of Route 66 in New Mexico," an oral
history project, https://storymaps.arcgis.com/stories/f1f3820170d24e
2ca79a2db31f5d9e76.

99   **attributed to Edward Beale**: Lewis Burt Lesley, ed., *Uncle Sam's Camels:
The Journal of May Humphreys Stacey Supplemented by the Report of Edward
Fitzgerald Beale (1857–1858)* (Harvard University Press, 1929), 121–22.

99   **living wayfinding markers**: for more on these trees, see Steve Houser et
al., *Comanche Marker Trees of Texas* (Texas A&M University Press, 2016).

100 **held a recent ceremony**: Torin Halsey, "Texas History: Comanche Nation
Marker Tree Dedicated in Ceremony, *Times Record News*, March 17, 2018.
https://www.timesrecordnews.com/story/news/local/2018/03/17/texas
-history-comanche-nation-marker-tree-dedicated-ceremony/433268002/.

101 **"We are part mineral . . . land"**: Robert Macfarlane, *Underland: A Deep
Time Journey* (Norton, 2019), 37.

102 **trail camera at Trapper's Point**: see http://www.trapperspoint.com/.

103 **"A wildlife crossing . . . wound"**: Trisha White to Catrin Einhorn,
in "How Do Animals Safely Cross a Highway? Take a Look," *New
York Times*, May 31, 2022. White also expressed enthusiasm for wildlife crossings, but wanted to contextualize it with the reality of habitat
fragmentation.

103 **a plan to decommission the Skyway**: see "NYS Route 5 (Buffalo Skyway)
Project," Transportation Project Report, New York State Department of
Transportation and US Department of Transportation Federal Highway
Administration, August 2020. For the wild plans for remaking the Skyway,
see Dave McKinley, "High Hopes: Skyway Redesign Competition Brings
Wide Array of Ideas," WGRZ, September 5, 2019.

103   **"what seems . . . origins"**: Georges Perec, "Approaches to What?," John Sturrock, trans., in *Species of Spaces and Other Pieces* (Penguin, 1997), 210.

104   **Cross Bronx Expressway**: Jane Holtz Kay, *Asphalt Nation: How the Automobile Took Over America, and How We Can Take It Back* (University of California Press, 1998), 230. The Cross Bronx Expressway (masterminded by Robert Moses) demolished 159 buildings, displacing five thousand people. At Love Canal, nine hundred families evacuated, and slightly more than six thousand people participated in a health study for former Love Canal residents.

104   **Miss Blacktop and Miss Concrete**: With thanks to my mother, Dolores Hayden, who first shared one of the photos with me from her own research into highways and suburbs. They are available via the Wisconsin Historical Society under "Dedication of Wisconsin's First Expressway."

105   **"With cataracts . . . indoors," "the colour of depth and distance"**: John Berger, "Raising the Portcullis: Some Notes After Having Cataracts Removed from My Eyes," *British Journal of General Practice*, 60:575, June 2010, https://doi.org/10.3399/bjgp10X509766.

105   **"it is as if . . . face"**: Berger, *And Our Faces*, 78.

7. If I'm Lonely

110   **the name Back Bay is literal**: see the chapter on Back Bay in Seasholes, *Gaining Ground*.

111   **fishweirs**: Seasholes, *Gaining Ground*, 187.

111   **over five thousand acres**: Seasholes, *Gaining Ground*, 2.

111   **"making water . . . invented property"**: Garrett Dash Nelson, "Making Water into Gold," Norman B. Leventhal Map and Education Center at the Boston Public Library, March 4, 2021, https://www.leventhalmap.org /articles/making-water-into-gold/.

111   **a fist that had been allowed to open**: Seasholes, *Gaining Ground*, 158.

112   **shit as well as wealth**: Seasholes, *Gaining Ground*, 172. See also Olmsted's description: "The water moving over it became exceedingly filthy so that even eels could not live in it. Then, as the water went out with the tide the mud was exposed to the sun, and a stench arose that became an insuf-

ferable nuisance to people living half a mile away," in his piece "Paper on the Back Bay Problem and Its Solution Read Before the Boston Society of Architects: A Jewel in Boston's Emerald Necklace, April 1886," in Charles E. Beveridge, ed., *Olmsted: Writings on Landscape, Culture, and Society* (Library of America, 2015), 620.

112 **"A greenish scum . . . mass below":** Committee report for the city of Boston, quoted in Seasholes, *Gaining Ground*, 172.

112 **discarded landscape, a sacrifice zone:** Orchid Tierney, "Materials Poetics: Landfills and Waste Management in Contemporary Literature and Media," dissertation, University of Pennsylvania, 2019.

113 **wrote that she was sleepwalking, "ludicrous":** Adrienne Rich, "Anger and Tenderness," in *Of Woman Born: Motherhood as Experience and Institution* (W. W. Norton, 1976), 26–27. See Maggie Doherty's excellent essay on Rich, "The Long Awakening of Adrienne Rich," *New Yorker*, November 23, 2020.

114 **"If I'm lonely . . . breath on the city":** Adrienne Rich, "Song," in *Diving into the Wreck: Poems, 1971–1972* (W. W. Norton, 2013), 20.

114 **acres of polluted mudflats:** Olmsted, "Paper on the Back Bay Problem," 618.

114 **refused to call the area a park, "improvement":** Witold Rybczynski, *A Clearing in the Distance: Frederick Law Olmsted and America in the 19th Century* (Scribner, 1999), 343.

115 **"If the state of Massachusetts," "eels could not live in it":** Olmsted, "Paper on the Back Bay Problem," 618, 620.

115 **"flowing mud":** Olmsted, "Paper on the Back Bay Problem," 618.

115 **the ha-ha:** The name for these ditches is first mentioned as "Ah! Ah!" to describe a ditch, "which surprises the eye upon coming near it," in A. J. Dézallier d'Argenville, John James, trans., *The Theory and Practice of Gardening: Wherein Is Fully Handled All That Telates to Fine Gardens, Commonly Called Pleasure-Gardens, as Parterres, Groves, Bowling-Greens &c.* (G. James, 1712), 77. For a more contemporary explanation, see Laurie Cluitmans, ed., *On the Necessity of Gardening* (Valiz, 2021), 89.

115 **the "unspoiled" kind:** for a good account of landscape architecture's problematic relationship to wilderness, see Miller, *This Radical Land*. See also Cronon, "The Trouble with Wilderness."

116 **trying to farm potatoes:** For a timeline and account of this early farm, see the personal papers collected in *Fredrick Law Olmsted, Landscape Architect, 1822–1903*, Frederick Law Olmsted Jr. and Theodora Kimball, eds., (Benjamin Blom, 1970), 5, 84.

117 **Olmsted toyed with names:** Justin Martin, *Genius of Place: The Life of Frederick Law Olmsted* (Da Capo Press, 2011), 337.

117 **bring "the wild" . . . those who could not travel:** Anne Whiston Spirn, "Constructing Nature: The Legacy of Frederick Law Olmsted," in William Cronon, ed., *Uncommon Ground: Toward Reinventing Nature* (W. W. Norton, 1995), 107.

117 **"The best result . . . natural state":** Olmsted, "Paper on the Back Bay Problem," 628.

118 **"the persistent . . . contribution":** Spirn, "Constructing Nature," 108.

118 **Fenway Victory Gardens:** see https://fenwayvictorygardens.org/history/.

119 **a process called homing:** for the best general explanation of this process see Merlin Sheldrake, *Entangled Life: How Fungi Make Our Worlds, Change Our Minds and Shape Our Futures* (Random House, 2020), 39.

119 **"Longing is never over . . . feel something":** Alina Ștefănescu interviewed by Ben Libman, *The Unnamable*, June 27, 2022, https://theunnamable.substack.com/p/interview-alina-stefanescu.

119 **community science surveys of insect biodiversity:** Christine Helie, "Collecting Treasure: Valuable Insect Data from the Field," April 8, 2019, https://fenwayvictorygardens.org/2019/04/08/collecting-treasure-valuable-insect-data-from-the-field/.

120 **Olmsted's park system:** Etienne Benson, "The Urbanization of the Eastern Gray Squirrel in the United States," *Journal of American History*, 100:3, December 2013, 696. See also Peter S. Alagona's chapter on eastern grays in *The Accidental Ecosystem: People and Wildlife in American Cities* (University of California Press, 2022).

120 **tens of millions of individual animals:** Alagona, *The Accidental Ecosystem*, 32.

120 **squirrels had permission:** Alagona, *The Accidental Ecosystem*, 32.

120 **"He should not go . . . thoughtless Sportsman":** Benjamin Franklin to Georgiana Shipley, September 26, 1772, *The Papers of Benjamin Franklin,*

vol. 19, January 1 through December 31, 1772, William B. Willcox, ed. (Yale University Press, 1975), 301–303.

121 **"I wish the bald eagle . . . robbing":** Benjamin Franklin to Sarah Bache, January 26, 1784, *The Papers of Benjamin Franklin, vol. 41, September 16, 1783, through February 29, 1784,* Ellen R. Cohn, ed. (Yale University Press, 2014), 503–511.

121 **squirrels in the mid-to-late 1800s:** Alagona, *The Accidental Ecosystem,* 32. See also Benson, 708.

122 **"the tameness . . . behavior toward nature":** Benson, "The Urbanization of the Eastern Gray Squirrel," 694.

122 **the food was often nutritionally poor:** Benson, "The Urbanization of the Eastern Gray Squirrel," 708.

122 **other species could survive:** Alagona, *The Accidental Ecosystem,* 41.

122 **"The conditions . . . maintaining them":** Benson, "The Urbanization of the Eastern Gray Squirrel," 696.

122 **"Eastern grays . . . would not be the last":** Alagona, *The Accidental Ecosystem,* 41.

123 **Ancient Fishweir Project:** see https://www.fishweir.org/.

123 **we continue to survive:** "The Massachusett Tribe at Ponkapoag," massachusetttribe.org.

123 **five-thousand-year-old fragments of fishweirs:** Seasholes, *Gaining Ground,* 187. See also Frederick Johnson, ed., *The Boylston Street Fishweir* (Papers of the Robert S. Peabody Foundation for Archaeology, 1942).

123 **"the ambiguity . . . citizen landscape altogether":** Mark Jarzombek, "The 'Indianized' Landscape of Massachusetts," *Places Journal,* February 2021, https://placesjournal.org/article/the-indianized-landscape-of -massachusetts/.

124 **after the Fens were finished:** Spirn, "Constructing Nature," 109–110.

124 **"waste of space":** see Bruno Rubio, "Fruits of Investigation," on the highlights of the Fenway Victory Gardens archives at the Massachusetts Historical Society, https://fenwayvictorygardens.org/2017/02/09/fruits -of-investigation/.

125 **"daylight" the river:** Kim A. O'Connell, "Mending the Necklace," *Landscape Architecture Magazine*, 91:7, July 2001, 38.

125 **talked the city engineer into:** Rybczynski, *A Clearing in the Distance*, 343.

126 **taking a hatchet to some ceiling beams:** see "Building Isabella's Museum" at https://www.gardnermuseum.org/about/building-isabellas-museum.

127 **"heighten our chances . . . dead rock":** Donna Jeanne Haraway, *Staying with the Trouble: Making Kin in the Chthulucene* (Duke University Press, 2016), 52.

8. The Echo

132 **drew manufacturing to the area:** on the development of hydropower and early industry around the falls, see Ginger Strand's chapter "King of Power, Queen of Beauty," in *Inventing Niagara: Beauty, Power, and Lies* (Simon & Schuster, 2008), 163. See also, Michael Zweig and Gordon Boyd, *The Federal Connection: A History of U.S. Military Involvement in the Toxic Contamination of Love Canal and the Niagara Frontier Region*, report for the New York State Assembly Task Force on Toxic Substances, January 21, 1981, 25.

132 **Model City:** Love's map for the proposed Model City is in the University at Buffalo Archives, and online at New York Heritage Digital Collections, https://cdm16694.contentdm.oclc.org/digital/collection/p16694coll1/id /1357/rec/.

132 **the rhetoric was progressive:** for more on the overlap between progressive talking points and ideas of industrial progress at Love Canal, see Richard S. Newman, "Making Love Canal," *Lapham's Quarterly*, July 13, 2016, https://www.laphamsquarterly.org/roundtable/making-love-canal.

133 *The War of Wealth:* see the poster, in the Library of Congress, with a representation of the exploding vault: https://www.loc.gov/item/2014636209.

133 **strange dump trucks that arrive by night:** interview in Chantal Calato's installation *Unseen*, Birchfield Penny Art Center, Buffalo, New York, 2020, https://www.unseen voices.com/. With thanks to the artist for allowing me to quote from the oral history interviews she collected.

133 **Lake Ontario Ordnance Works:** "Lake Ontario Ordnance Works," US Army Corps of Engineers, Buffalo District Website, https://www.lrb .usace.army.mil/Missions/HTRW/DERP-FUDS/Lake-Ontario-Ordnance -Works/.

133   **1,500 acres were transferred:** "Lake Ontario Ordnance Works."

133   **"storage . . . atomic bomb":** "Lake Ontario Ordnance Works."

133   **made a fortune:** Keith O'Brien, *Paradise Falls* (Pantheon, 2022), 45.

133   **"the 'Poison Gas King' of America":** O'Brien, *Paradise Falls.*

134   **Disposing of waste was a problem:** Strand, *Inventing Niagara,* 178–179.

134   **fifty dollars apiece:** Strand, *Inventing Niagara,* 178–179.

134   **Hooker got permission:** Zweig and Boyd, *The Federal Connection,* 29.

134   **employee at the edge with a hose:** O'Brien, *Paradise Falls,* 46–47.

134   **weighing competing forces:** O'Brien, *Paradise Falls,* 48, and Zweig and Boyd, *The Federal Connection,* 30–31.

135   **"The day of reckoning . . . someone else":** Adeline Gordon Levine, *Love Canal: Science, Politics, and People* (Lexington Books, 1982), 2.

136   **piled up on the ice:** Gene Warner, "The Blizzard of '77: Buffalo's Storm for the Ages," *Buffalo News,* January 22, 2017.

136   **Federal Emergency Management Agency:** see Timothy W. Kneeland's account of the full story of the blizzard and FEMA in his book *Declaring Disaster: Buffalo's Blizzard of '77 and the Creation of FEMA* (Syracuse University Press, 2021).

136   **the Comprehensive Environmental...Act:** see the Summary of the Comprehensive Environmental Response, Compensation, and Liability Act (Superfund) 42 U.S.C. §9601 et seq. (1980), US Environmental Protection Agency, https://www.epa.gov/laws-regulations/summary -comprehensive-environmental-response-compensation-and-liability-act. The model of taxing polluters to keep CERCLA funded has now lapsed, though bills before Congress have recently tried to reinstate it.

136   **returning her twins' sneakers:** Lindsey Gruson, "Home to Some Is Still Love Canal to Others," *New York Times,* December 9, 1991.

136   **Lois Gibbs:** the so-called "Mother of the Superfund." For an account of the beginnings of her activism, see her book *Love Canal: My Story* (Grove Press, 1982), 9. For her, awareness of the dump began with Michael Brown's reporting for the *Niagara Falls Gazette.*

137   **Agnes Jones and Elene Thornton:** for a full account of the Concerned Love Canal Renters Association, see Elizabeth D. Blum, *Love Canal*

Revisited: Race, Class, and Gender in Environmental Activism (University of Kansas Press, 2008), especially her chapter on race and environmental injustice. Many of the women in the Renters Association tied their activism directly to principles of the civil rights movement.

137 **"severe sewer defects"**: Blum, *Love Canal Revisited*, 75.

137 **"When you can hear . . . too late"**: Levine, *Love Canal*, 58.

137 **"The clay strata . . . condition"**: Health Commissioner Whalen, Love Canal Health Department Orders, June 20, 1978, University at Buffalo Archives, Box 1, Folder 33.

137 **storm sewers**: Stephen Lester's daily reports contain multiple mentions, for example, see report dated October 26, 1979, Lois Gibbs Love Canal Papers, Tufts Archival Research Center, Box 5, Folder 13. See also Gibbs's early account of the smells from storm sewer opening in *My Story*, 40.

138 **ride the school bus, "He was an outcast"**: Chantal Calato, interview with the author, May 27, 2022.

139 **remembered the fires**: Zweig and Boyd, *The Federal Connection*, 43.

139 **Beverly Paigen, "housewife data"**: Gibbs, *My Story*, 67, 82.

140 **conflict of interest**: interview with Beverly Paigen for Lynn Corcoran in the documentary film *In Our Own Backyard: The First Love Canal Connection*, University at Buffalo Archives, Box 1.

140 **patriotic pride in their wartime work**: Strand, *Inventing Niagara*, 253.

140 **pruning the shrubs**: see the story of the Buteras in Peter Simon's account for *Buffalo News*, May 13, 1990, A-12.

140 **renters faced discrimination**: Thomas Fletcher, "Neighborhood Change at Love Canal: Contamination, Evacuation and Resettlement," *Land Use Policy*, 19:4, October 2002, 311–323.

141 **"Fuck . . . carcinogenosphere"**: Boyer, *The Undying*, 78.

142 **the "confluence"**: Luella Kenny, talk at Burning Books, Buffalo, NY, June 6, 2022.

143 **her youngest son, Jon Allen's**: Luella Kenny, interview with the author, July 8, 2022. For more on his story, see O'Brien's detailed account of his illness in *Paradise Falls*.

143   **idiopathic:** Jon Allen Kenny, autopsy report, 1979. Courtesy of Luella Kenny.

143   **bird had collapsed and died:** Kenny described this event in her talk. See also Stephen Lester's daily report for June 7, 1979, Lois Gibbs Love Canal Papers, Tufts Archival Research Center, Box 5, Folder 13.

143   **"I mean . . . long time ago" and subsequent quotes from Luella Kenny:** Luella Kenny, talk at Burning Books, Buffalo, NY, June 6, 2022.

144   **"8/20/79 . . . the house":** Luella Kenny, "Log of Outfall at 96th and Greenwald," 1979, Kenny's personal papers, with thanks to Luella for her permission to quote. I've presented several partial entries here.

144   **LCARA:** LCARA meeting minutes, December 21, 1982, University at Buffalo Archives, Box 7, Folder 3.

145   **the question of "habitability":** LCARA meeting minutes.

145   **porch lights:** these come up a few times in the LCARA meeting minutes, particularly on February 12, 1992, University at Buffalo Archives, Box 7, Folder 15.

145   **the health commissioner ruled:** Commissioner David Axelrod, "Love Canal Emergency Declaration Area: Decision on Habitability," New York State Department of Health, September 1988, 3–4.

146   **"to have any market value . . . environmental liens":** "Final Generic Environmental Impact Statement for Love Canal Area Master Plan," prepared for LCARA, 19.

146   **packet of disclosures:** LCARA sales materials, 1992, University at Buffalo Archives, Box 11, folder 9. Ironically, one of the documents in the disclosure packet was the EPA's reply to Lois Gibbs's letter of protest when resettlement began.

146   **"use the subjective approach . . . echo":** O'Laughlin to the LCARA board, LCARA meeting minutes, 1982, University at Buffalo Archives, Box 7, Folder 3.

147   **her personal geography entangles:** Chantal Calato, "Love Built My Rainbow," August 9, 2020, https://www.unseen-voices.com/behind -unseen/2019/11/14/love-built-my-rainbow.

147   the Niagara Falls Storage Site: "About the Niagara Falls Storage Site,"
       US Army Corps of Engineers, Buffalo District Website, https://www.lrb
       .usace.army.mil/Missions/HTRW/FUSRAP/Niagara-Falls-Storage-Site/.

147   "the danger . . . chain-link fence": Calato, "Love Built."

148   "We are not above . . . ecological reciprocity": Lisa Wells, *Believers:
       Making a Life at the End of the World* (Farrar, Straus and Giroux, 2021), 266.

150   *Unseen* and all quotes from the installation in this chapter: Calato,
       Unseen.

152   "Move-in ready . . . water access": sales listing for 1064 Ninety-Sixth
       Street, Niagara Falls, New York, https://www.realtor.com/realestateand
       homes-detail/1064-96th-St_Niagara-Falls_NY_14304_M35429-59530
       (there's even a picture of the creek itself).

152   "in perpetuity": Michele DeLuca, "Safe or Not, Love Canal Remains in
       Perpetuity," *Lockport Union-Sun & Journal*, August 8, 2018.

153   field office in the area: Strand, *Inventing Niagara*, 225.

153   secret development of the bomb: Strand, *Inventing Niagara*, 225.

153   Hooker Chemical handled uranium ores: Zweig and Boyd, *The Federal
       Connection*, 89–90.

153   Linde Air Products: Zweig and Boyd, *The Federal Connection*, 126. The
       company is now called Linde.

153   with the explicit knowledge of the army: Zweig and Boyd, *The Federal
       Connection*, 126–129.

153   "cleanup and consolidation": "About the Niagara Falls Storage Site,"
       US Army Corps of Engineers.

154   "dumping . . . different purposes": Zweig and Boyd, *The Federal
       Connection*, viii–ix.

154   dumping drums at Love Canal: Zweig and Boyd, *The Federal Connection*,
       29, 40–42.

155   division between a first and second body: Daisy Hildyard, *The Second
       Body* (Fitzcarraldo Editions, 2018), 19–20.

156   Tifft Nature Preserve: David J. Spiering, "Tifft Nature Preserve
       Management Plan," February 2009.

158 **nearly a quarter of people:** The EPA reports that roughly 22 percent of people in the United States live within three miles of a Superfund site, or 73 million people. Environmental Protection Agency, Office of Land and Emergency Management, 2020.

158 **116 chemical drums:** Spiering, "Tifft Management Plan," 9.

159 **without ever hearing the story:** see the story of George Kreutz in Erika Engelhaupt, "Happy Birthday, Love Canal," *Environmental Science and Technology*, November 13, 2008, https://doi.org/10.1021/es802376z. Chantal and Luella also mentioned people who have moved to these areas without knowing about their toxic legacy.

160 *much unseen is also here*: Walt Whitman, "Song of the Open Road," *Leaves of Grass*.

9. The Shadow Count

162 **"It is not possible . . . loneliness":** Barry Lopez, *Embrace Fearlessly the Burning World* (Random House, 2022), 69.

163 **Bachman's warbler:** Several writers have pointed out the drawbacks of naming animals after humans, especially after early naturalists like John James Audubon and his friend John Bachman, who both owned slaves and defended the practice of slavery. It feels wrong to preserve their names in a list of species, and to saddle them onto the life of a bird. For more on this, see Arianna Remmel, "What's in a Bird Name?," *Audubon*, summer 2022, https://www.audubon.org/magazine/summer-2022/whats-bird-name.

163 **"the rarest North American songbird":** Roger Tory Peterson, *A Field Guide to the Birds East of the Rockies* (Houghton Mifflin, 1980), 242.

163 **last sightings of Bachman's warblers:** "Removal of 23 Extinct Species from the Lists of Endangered and Threatened Wildlife and Plants," Fish and Wildlife Service, Department of the Interior, *Federal Register*, 86:187, September 30, 2021, 54302–3.

164 **166 hours:** "Bachman's Warbler Searches at Congaree National Park," National Park Service: https://www.nps.gov/rlc/ogbfrec/bachmans.htm.

164 **"delist" this warbler:** Fish and Wildlife Service, "Removal of 23 Extinct Species from the Lists of Endangered and Threatened Wildlife and Plants."

164   *common bird in steep decline*: see the Partners in Flight category here
https://partnersinflight.org/conservation_concern/common-steep-decline/.

164   **lost nearly three billion birds:** Kenneth V. Rosenberg et al., "Decline of
the North American Avifauna," *Science*, 366:6461, September 19, 2019,
https://www.science.org/doi/10.1126/science.aaw1313.

164   **half-life:** defined by Partners in Flight as the "estimated number of
years until 50% of the remaining population is lost, based on recent
10-year Breeding Bird Survey trend" (the breeding bird survey is a
community science survey that takes place in the spring). See https://pif
.birdconservancy.org/ACAD/Database.aspx.

165   **the count began in 1900:** see "History of the Christmas Bird Count,"
https://www.audubon.org/conservation/history-christmas-bird-count.

165   **"hie them to the fields . . . path":** Frank Chapman, "A Christmas Bird
Census," *Bird-Lore*, vol. 2, December 1900, 192.

171   **"as children . . . father's face":** Peter Marris, unpublished memoir, 2006.

172   **"the grammar of animacy,":** Kimmerer, *Braiding Sweetgrass*, 55.

172   **"To be a hill . . . alive," "Water, land . . . mushrooms," "A bay . . .
dead":** Kimmerer, *Braiding Sweetgrass*, 54–55.

173   **"The arrogance . . . human," "Saying 'it' makes . . . 'natural resources'":** Kimmerer, *Braiding Sweetgrass*, 56–57.

173   **the true expansiveness:** for more on animal perception, see Ed Yong's
beautiful *An Immense World: How Animal Senses Reveal the Hidden Realms
Around Us* (Random House, 2022). For plants, see Kimmerer, "White Pine."

173   **clock and compass:** Van Doren, interview with the author, April 7, 2022.

173   **nocturnal restlessness:** Cas Eikenaar et al., "Migratory Restlessness in
Captive Individuals Predicts Actual Departure in the Wild," *Biology Letters*,
10:4, April 1, 2014, https://doi.org/10.1098/rsbl.2014.0154.

173   **Beyond that first instinctive journey:** Rachel Muheim et al., "Polarized
Light Cues Underlie Compass Calibration in Migratory Songbirds," *Science*,
313:5788, August 11, 2006, 837, https://www.science.org/doi/10.1126
/science.1129709.

177   **Christmas Bird Count route:** to sign up for a route or see the route maps
in your area, see https://www.audubon.org/conservation/join-christmas

-bird-count. To see data from previous counts, visit https://netapp.audubon
.org/CBCObservation/CurrentYear/ResultsByCount.aspx.

179 **"archivists of soundscapes," "compelling proof . . . next"**: Ana Dalziell,
quoted in Jennifer Ackerman, *The Bird Way: A New Look at How Birds Talk,
Work, Play, Parent, and Think* (Penguin Press, 2020), 82. I'm also grateful
to Geoff Manaugh, "Acoustic Archaeology," *BLDGBLOG*, December 28,
2020, https://bldgblog.com/tag/lyrebirds/.

Acknowledgments

Thanks, first and foremost, to those who took the time to share their worlds with me over the course of writing these essays—Nona Bloomer, Joel Helander, and Scott Gordon on the history of Lost Lake; Jennifer Mattei and Deanna Broderick with Project Limulus; Carla Dove and Faridah Dahlan at the Feather Identification Lab; Benjamin Van Doren at the Cornell Lab of Ornithology; Travis DeVault for his expertise on human-wildlife collisions in the air and on the ground; Phyllis Willmott for the gift of my father's road trip postcards; Jon Hitchcock at the National Weather Service in Buffalo for the storm-spotter training; Chantal Calato and Luella Kenny for trusting me with their stories; Jessica Hollister for all her help with the Love Canal archives at the University at Buffalo, and Pamela S. M. Hopkins at the Tufts Archival Research Center; Bethany Sheffer and the Mikes in Sharon and Cornwall, especially Mike Redmond, whose long memory of both people and birds has helped to preserve my father's presence there.

I am grateful to the research and writing of the following experts, whose published work has helped inform my own: Deborah Cramer and William Sargent on horseshoe crabs, Nancy Seasholes on landmaking in Boston, Peter S. Alagona on squirrels, Elizabeth D. Blum, Keith O'Brien, and Ginger Strand on Niagara Falls, Robin Wall Kimmerer on loneliness and language.

I particularly want to acknowledge the legacies of biologist Jennifer Mattei, who died in 2023 just as this book was going to press, and who worked tirelessly to study the decline of the Long Island Sound horseshoe crab population; and of Don Kenyon, my father-in-law, who died in 2021 just as I was finishing the first draft, and whose encouragement meant so much. His kindness and curiosity will be missed.

My deepest gratitude to everyone at Graywolf, and especially to Anni Liu and Chantz Erolin for giving this book a home and treating it with such perceptiveness and care. Reading your comments has been an enduring gift. Thanks to Fiona McCrae for beginning the conversation, and to Katie Dublinski for helping to turn a manuscript into a book.

Deep appreciation to my agent, Ian Bonaparte, for not just entertaining but also championing an idea that could not be easily categorized. I'm lucky to be working with you.

I am grateful to the Robert B. Silvers Foundation for a Grant for Work in Progress that helped provide vital support and encouragement for finishing this book. Thanks to Paul Vanouse and the Coalesce Center for Biological Art, where I was a writer in residence in the first year of working on this book. A MacDowell Fellowship provided transformative support in a very difficult time—thank you for the gift of joy in work, and for letting me return. Many sections of this book benefitted from being written and revised in the clear light of those New Hampshire woods.

Thanks to Hayden Bennett at the *Believer* for publishing an early version of "Extremotolerance."

Thank you, Caitlin Van Dusen, for the thoughtful copyedit. And thank you to Rachel Garner, who fact-checked this book with an eagle eye.

To the friends and mentors and teachers who have encouraged my writing (many of whom also advised Matt and me through our attempts to find jobs in the same place), Susan Howe, Dave Bercovici, Robert Pinsky, Louise Glück, Hazel Carby, Bonnie Costello, Alice Kaplan—your support has meant more than you know.

Thanks to the friends who read and commented on all or part of the manuscript in progress—Virginia Eubanks for putting exactly the right book in my hands, Summer J. Hart for sharing bird lore and dark humor, Dave Alff for perceptive comments and appreciation of Logan airport, Julia Dzwonkoski for snow walks (in the most joyful snowsuit) when I was stuck, Elisa Gonzalez for reading a very early version of the horseshoe crab essay and telling me it needed to be expanded, and Lauren Roberts for encouraging early experiments with structure. I am especially grateful to Jen Kabat, who has read every word of this book several times over, and whose kindness and generosity have made the work so much less lonely. Thank you for being in the process with me.

To those friends and family inside and outside Buffalo who took the time to listen, or offer encouragement, or answer questions along the way—Sue Kenyon, Becky Brown and Bill Santen, David Herzberg and Erin Hatton, Katie Rowan, Tony O'Rourke and Christine Varnado, Aaron Bartley, Elizabeth Meg Williams, Kyla Kegler, Dalia Antonia Caraballo Muller, Mark Shepard and Antonina Simeti, Emma Tessler, Nell Stevens, Carina del Valle Schorske, and Adam Dalva—I appreciate you so much. Thanks to Penelope Creeley for giving us the best possible landing in Buffalo. And thanks to Elvi Jo Dougherty, Pip, and Soliegh for being our forever neighbors.

To my mother, Dolores Hayden, thank you for all that you have shared with me, even in the deep spaces of grief where sharing is not intuitive. Thank you for telling me your stories, for believing that I could someday write mine.

To my father, Peter Marris, whose teaching runs through this book yet always holds more than words can say, whose love for the world was and is a revelation—thank you for giving me what I needed, before I even understood how much.

To Matt Kenyon, who read every scrap and version and draft—your brilliance and love have been an astonishing light. Thank you for being with me in the thicket of metaphors, for making a home in life and art—it means the world to me.

LAURA MARRIS is a writer and translator. She is a MacDowell fellow and the recipient of a Silvers Grant for Work in Progress. Her recent translations include Albert Camus's *The Plague* and *To Live Is to Resist*, a biography of Antonio Gramsci. Books she has translated have been shortlisted for the Oxford-Weidenfeld Translation Prize, the Scott Moncrieff Prize, and the French-American Foundation Translation Prize. She teaches creative writing at the University at Buffalo.

The text of *The Age of Loneliness* is set in Bembo MT Pro.
Book design by Rachel Holscher.
Composition by Bookmobile Design and Digital
Publisher Services, Minneapolis, Minnesota.
Manufactured by Friesens on acid-free,
100 percent postconsumer wastepaper.